TEACHING PIANO
Adventures®

by Nancy and Randall Faber
with Marienne Uszler

PIANO ADVENTURES®

ISBN 978-1-61677-631-2

Table of Contents

Icon Legend |  Teacher Manual
Duet Appendix
(this book, pp. 140-203)

Accompaniment on
Compact Disc
(sold separately, CD1001)

The Piano Adventures Teacher

To the student, Piano Adventures implies an exciting exploration. To the teacher, Piano Adventures implies a mission and mindset which puts the student's personal development in the fore. The Piano Adventures Teacher refers to a philosophy of teaching, not just to the choice of method materials.

Attitude

The Piano Adventures philosophy puts the student first—before the music, pedagogy, or performance goals.

■ The spotlight is on the individual student's growth.

■ The goal is to awaken in students the awe of music as an art, being always mindful that music study should enhance and not hinder self-esteem.

■ We enrich students by revealing the musical artistry within them and by developing their skills for all kinds of musical expression.

We believe that our students can be our teachers. We have a profound respect for the process of teaching.

Multiple Outcomes

Most of us grow to recognize the potential for deep influence on our students' personal development. Piano study can be a vehicle for fostering a host of valuable life skills that lie outside the realm of musical skill. While the focus of a lesson is to develop musical proficiency, we also have the opportunity to nurture other positive characteristics.

■ Confidence

■ Curiosity

■ Discipline

■ Patience

■ Self-esteem

■ Sensitivity to nuance

■ Understanding how process relates to product

■ Work habits

The Piano Adventures Teacher believes that developing pianistic skill is a powerful way to affect a young person's attitude and character for future endeavors.

The Piano Adventures Teacher
Believes passionately
that music enriches
life.

Teaching Process

It is necessary to recognize that fun is an important motivator for children. In fact, the need for pleasure and fun carries into all ages. Consequently, early piano study should be conducted with a spirit of play. This does not imply inefficiency or ineffectiveness. To the contrary. A spirit of play in the lesson engages the attention and energy of the student, promoting deeper learning. The degree of student participation predicts the degree of musical absorption and application.

The Piano Adventures Teacher invites student talk. The relationship and the dialogue between student and teacher can provide:

- A foundation for stimulating musical growth

- A platform for addressing elements of motivation that may arise

- A vehicle for developing valued life skills

We engage the student with a sense of adventure and discovery. There is purpose and direction in the lesson and lots of hard work. But discipline can be rewarding when one's attention and senses are actively engaged. This blurring between "work" and "fun" is precisely intended as it leads to deep learning, effective practice habits, and a healthy work ethic.

Teaching Materials

A discussion of The Piano Adventures Teacher would be incomplete without mention of teaching materials because the choice of music and method can dramatically influence the success of piano lessons.

The teacher, the student, the parent, and the choice of music form the essential building blocks. For the teacher, the method offers a musical highway on which to travel. For the student, each musical mile traveled well increases pianistic skill. Consequently, the importance of the music and method of learning cannot be overstated. They are vital in retaining student interest and creating a sense of achievement.

A good teacher chooses teaching materials wisely and knows how to teach the materials thoroughly —analytically, creatively, expressively. This enables the teacher to exploit the strengths of each student's learning style while simultaneously stimulating less-developed learning areas.

The Piano Adventures Teacher

- Involves the student in the purpose of the curriculum as they travel through the course.

- Intervenes appropriately when a skill falters or motivation flags through a combination of patience, listening, innovation, and enthusiasm.

- Provides helpful feedback, physical modeling, and personalized supplementary materials that celebrate individual student interest.

Leading to Reading

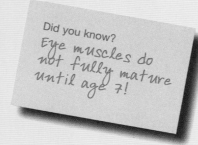

We can make music without learning to read music. So why do piano teachers put so much emphasis on note reading?

Reading music gives ...

- Another "language"
- A chance to play or sing whatever you like
- A way to communicate with other players or singers
- A way to share music you compose
- A mode for communicating complex art music

Reading symbols ...

- Stimulates neural networking within the brain
- Helps you solve problems
- Arouses curiosity
- Provides clues to other cultures
- Intensifies poise and self-worth

Pictures, gestures, and speech prepare us to read our native language. Similar experiences prepare one to read music.

The natural learning sequence

Experience first	Names later
See and touch your toes ⟶	"toes"
Reach above your head ⟶	"up"
Feel an ice cube ⟶	"cold"
Hold and play with a ball ⟶	"ball"
See (many) dogs ⟶	"dog"

The learning sequence in music

First	Then learn
Listen to music ⟶	Soft/loud, Up/down, Fast/slow
Feel rhythms ⟶	Note values
Play music ⟶	Notation
Recognize patterns ⟶	How to compare and describe them
Create music ⟶	Ways to write it

Did you know?
Eye muscles do not fully mature until age 7!

The Challenge: Sensory Overload

Pianists have a lot to think about: correct posture, large muscle use, small muscle control, coordination, and complex musical notation. This poses a special problem for beginning piano students. Like an over-watered flower garden, the beginning student's attention may become "saturated"—overwhelmed by too many concurrent, challenging stimuli.

It is not at all surprising that something has to "overflow". Indeed, beginning students commonly exhibit problems with tension or faulty basic technique when their attention is wholly absorbed by music notation. Sometimes students play unmusically or are insensitive to wrong notes because attention to reading distracts them from listening.

The language we call music notation is a rich mosaic, conveying a wealth of specific instructions to the player: Which key do I play? How long should I hold it? How loud? How should I play the note in relationship to others surrounding it? What finger and hand should I use? Are there ways to initially simplify this language so the student may gradually develop reading skill without the consequences of overtaxing a beginner's attention?

The Solution: Pre-reading

Just as training wheels aid a child learning to ride a bike, pre-reading introduces beginning students to reading notes. Pre-reading notes do not appear on the music staff, and note names are placed inside the note heads. The notes are carefully placed on the page to show the contour (shape) of the melody, thus stressing directional (up and down) reading.

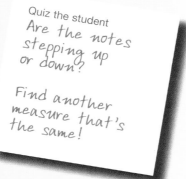

Quiz the student
Are the notes stepping up or down?

Find another measure that's the same!

Pre-reading teaches ...

Conceptual Skills

- ◼ Steady pulse
- ◼ Read note values
- ◼ Read directionally
- ◼ Recognize patterns

Motor Skills

- ◼ Differentiate left and right hands
- ◼ Track with the eyes from left to right
- ◼ Place hands on the correct keys
- ◼ Equate stepwise movement with adjacent fingers, skips with non-adjacent fingers

Musical Skills

- ◼ Listen
- ◼ Feel rhythm
- ◼ Correlate notation and performance
- ◼ Memorize by pattern
- ◼ Create

Don't be fooled!

Pre-reading is not a delay of reading "real music". It is a rich opportunity to shape conceptual and musical development through engaging all the senses and intellect in appropriate and compelling ways.

Group lesson—3:30pm

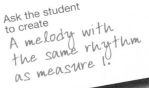

Ask the student to create A melody with the same rhythm as measure 1!

Sitting at the Piano

Lesson Book page 4

what's new

- Where to sit on the bench
- Sitting tall on the bench
- Measuring the distance from the fallboard

what's important

- Correct posture
- Appropriate seating distance
- Arms level with the keyboard

studio supplies

- For correct seating height, students may use cushions
- For foot support and pedaling, students may benefit from:
  - a foot stand
  - commercial pedal extensions
  - a turned-over box or crate

let's get started

1 A piano bench has no back or arms. Sit on the front half so you can lean to the left or right.

2 Measure the distance between you and the piano: put your arms straight out from your body, closing your hands to make loose fists.

3 Your knuckles should just touch the fallboard. That's how you measure the distance between you and the piano.

4 Put your loose fists on the keys. Your elbows should hang loosely and your back should be straight.

5 Are you sitting tall?

Measure distance from the keyboard with a "Karate pose".

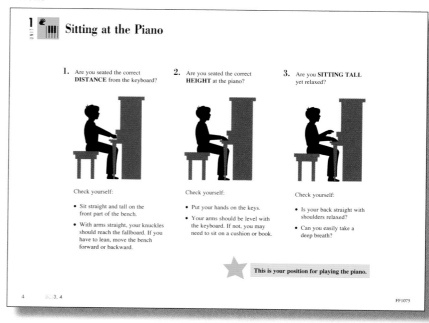

explore & create

■ **Paper Towel Holder**

If I wanted to blow through a paper towel holder, it would have to be straight to let the air go through. (Provide a paper towel holder and look through it.)

The towel holder is like your windpipe. To let the air flow through, sit tall! If you slump, the air can't pass easily through your body. (Bend the paper towel holder and attempt to look through it again.)

■ **You and the Bench**

(Rearrange the bench so that it's crooked, too far, or too close.) Let's see you find how you should move the bench to sit at the piano.

■ **New Terms**

Find and touch what I ask for:
Piano legs
Fallboard
Keyboard
Your forearms

 *Make good posture a good habit!*

pedagogy pointers

Sitting at the piano is not like sitting on a chair at home—and even there children often slouch or scrunch because most home furniture is not child-size. It's important, therefore, to demonstrate and explain proper posture.

There are easy and sure-fire ways to measure where and how to sit in relation to the piano and to the keyboard. Measurements will change as each child develops, but the process of learning to adjust to the instrument is guided by basic principles. Best to learn these at the beginning.

Sitting properly at the keyboard affects so much else—whether you can breathe with ease, whether you are relaxed, whether your feet give you the necessary support, and whether you are "centered" on the end of your spine.

Poor seating position or poor posture is the root of many technical problems. Right from the start make good posture a good habit.

PIANO ADVENTURES VIDEO

see it in action

Teaching Video 1

Olivia sits properly on the edge of the bench, but she discovers she's too far away. With arms straight out, her knuckles don't touch the fallboard! Moving the bench solves the problem.

When her hands lift up to the keys, she learns to measure distance by checking her arms. If you sit tall on the bench, your arms can fly to each end of the keyboard, and you can lean left and right.

Each of those different-sized players finds just the right distance and height. Ready to play!

Ask Yourself

■ What is the importance of the approach to and from the keyboard?

■ Although there is no direct attention given to the placement of the feet, do you think these students feel firmly centered on the bench?

Making a Round Hand Shape

Lesson Book page 5

INTRODUCTION

what's new

- **Open and closed hand**
- **Curved fingers**
- **Flexible wrist**

what's important

- **Making a round hand shape**
- **Using a flexible wrist**

studio supplies

■ These items may come in handy to promote a round hand shape:

- a tiny racecar
- a cotton ball

It's easier to set the standard at the outset than to undo bad habits later.

let's get started

1 Put your left (or right) hand straight out in front of you. Which finger is the longest? The shortest?

2 We can do a magic trick to make all the fingers the same length. (Demonstrate a curved hand position.)

3 Curve your fingers to make a C. Now your fingertips are in a line. Magic!

4 Imagine you're holding a small round apple over the keys. Drop the apple gently. Now wave goodbye to the keys. Let your wrists flop.

explore & create

■ **Open-Close**
Open and close your hand into a C shape in rhythm. I'll play some music while we say Open-Close. (Teacher Duet)

Making a Round Hand Shape

1. Hold your hands out with fingers straight. Notice the fingers are all different lengths.

2. Now relax and **round the hand**. *Magic!* Your fingers are all the same length.

round hand shape
Notice your hand forms the letter C for "correct."

Hand Shape Warm-up

3. Open, then close your fingers to a round hand shape. Do it several times. Say, "Open, closed," etc.

Now continue the motions in rhythm with the duet!

Wrist Warm-up

4. Gently flop your wrists down (and up) with a **round hand shape**. Pretend to shake water drops off your fingertips.

Teacher Duet: (Student does *open-closed* motions in rhythm to the music.)

mf
Say, "Open," Closed," Open," Closed," Open," Closed," Open," Closed!"

Teacher Note: This duet allows the student to practice an open and round hand shape to a steady beat.

FF1075

3, 4   5

partner pages

Technique & Artistry
p. 3 What is Technique?

Piano technique means skill. This page compares piano technique to a basketball player dribbling and a ballerina leaping. Piano technique uses the muscles of the fingers, wrists, arms, and torso.

p. 4 Five Secrets for Piano Technique

The opening pages of this book show five technique secrets for this level. These are used as warm-ups throughout the book.

- Karate Pose helps establish good posture at the piano. The student may do Karate Pose at each lesson to correct slouching or sitting too close.

- Blooming Flowers uses the image of a bud slowly opening to a rounded hand shape. The student may do this easily at any time during the lesson to reestablish a good hand position.

- These technique secrets will be used throughout the book. The two secrets in T & A, p. 4 may be introduced at any time during the Lesson Book Unit 1, pp. 4-13.

pedagogy pointers

Developing a curved, natural, and relaxed hand position is an important first step in shaping a student's technique.

It will take many reminders before this hand shape becomes second nature, but the sooner the process is begun, the better the chance of succeeding.

It is far easier to set the standard at the outset than to undo bad habits later.

It is equally important to help a student develop a flexible wrist. Analogies like waving goodbye or shaking drops off the fingertips are easy ways to introduce this concept.

Gentle reminders combined with careful observation (on your part) will help foster a natural flexibility.

PIANO ADVENTURES VIDEO

see it in action

Teaching Video 2

Our fingers are all different lengths, so we need a way to make them equal over the keys. If your hands form the letter C, they'll be in a soft, round shape and your fingertips will all line up. Patrick discovers this simple magic trick and can quickly see that it works. With a steady, cheerful accompaniment to make it fun and musical, he can play the Open-Close game.

Pretending to drop something onto the keys releases the wrist so it can flop. Waving to the keys is another gesture that encourages the hands to "hang loose". Patrick's on his way to being a "natural".

Ask Yourself

- What does Patrick do after he shapes his left hand for the first time?

- What do you notice about the teacher's activities?

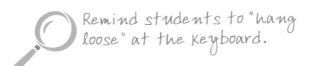

Remind students to "hang loose" at the keyboard.

Finger Numbers

Lesson Book page 6

what's new

- **Which is the left hand? Which is the right?**
- **Finger numbers in each hand**

what's important

- **Distinguishing left from right hand**
- **Using each finger, in each hand, as called**

let's get started

1 Let's trace your hands. Which is your left hand? Which is your right?

2 Let's number the fingers in each hand. (Begin with the left hand.)

3 Put your hands together, fingertips touching. Tap the fingers I call out.

Children often forget which hand is which.

explore & create

- **Stick 'em up!**
  (On the traced hands) Paste a sticker over the finger that I ask for. Be sure to use the correct hand!

- **Rings Around the Fingers**
  (Have a selection of rings ready.) Put a ring on the hand and finger I call out.

  (See Video)

- **Rings Away!**
  (Have rings on all the fingers.) Take the ring off each finger I call out.

  (See Video)

- **Tap Time**
  (On the fallboard or a table) Tap fingers number two … four … one. Don't forget—tap on the tips!

- **Tricky Tap Time**
  (On fallboard or table)
  Left hand, finger three …
  Right hand, finger one …
  Left hand, finger five …

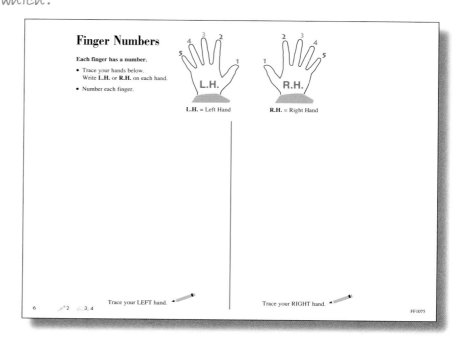

Finger Numbers

Each finger has a number.

- Trace your hands below.
  Write **L.H.** or **R.H.** on each hand.
- Number each finger.

L.H.

R.H.

L.H. = Left Hand   **R.H.** = Right Hand

Trace your LEFT hand.   Trace your RIGHT hand.

6   2   3, 4   FF1075

partner pages

Theory
p. 2 Which Hand and Finger?

- The student identifies left hand or right hand and circles finger 1 2 3 4 or 5.

Technique & Artistry
pp. 4-5 Five Secrets for Piano Technique

- Making O's presents firm fingertips. The student makes an "O" by gently pressing the fingertip and thumb together. Different finger combinations are used: 2-1, 3-1, 4-1, and 5-1.

- Heavy Wet Ropes introduces arm weight by bringing the arms up in slow motion and dropping completely relaxed into the lap. This encourages students to be aware of the weight of their arms, as well as the tips of their fingers.

- Thumb Perch addresses wrist position through the angle of the thumb. Perching on the side tip keeps the wrist from sagging, and helps guarantee a round hand shape.

- These three secrets may be introduced at any time during the Lesson Book Unit 1, pp. 4-13.

pedagogy pointers

Which hand is which? Children often forget.

They love to have their hands traced, and that's a good way to help them distinguish.

Since success at the keyboard involves playing with specific hands, as well as with both hands, knowing left from right must become second nature.

Finger numbers can be mixed up, too, especially in the left hand where finger number one is the thumb.

Tapping opposite matching pairs is an easy way to begin identifying and testing finger numbers because isometric activity is easy and natural.

When the hands are separated, responding with the correct finger can be more challenging.

PIANO ADVENTURES VIDEO

see it in action

Teaching Video 3

When Hannah puts her hands together with fingertips touching, it's easy to see how the finger numbers match up. And who doesn't like to paste on stickers? Remember—ask first for the hand, then the finger. Taking rings on and off is a stylish way to check out those hands and fingers. You can see Hannah sizing up the "jewels". Rings on her fingers! (We'll skip the bells on the toes for now …)

Ask Yourself

- Could you invent some finger games that a student could play with eyes closed?

- What would be some advantages of playing finger games with eyes closed?

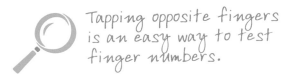

Tapping opposite fingers is an easy way to test finger numbers.

Finger Flashcards

Lesson Book page 7

what's new

- **Playing fingers in succession**
- **Often-used finger patterns**

what's important

- **Playing finger patterns in a steady rhythm**
- **Playing finger patterns with a rounded hand shape**

let's get started

1 Get your fingers moving! Here are six flashcards with peppy patterns for each hand.

2 (Fingers on the fallboard or a table) Let's try Flashcard 1. Which hand? Four times around. Say the numbers!

1 2 3 4	1 2 3 4
1 2 3 4	1 2 3 4

3 Here goes Flashcard 2 … 3 … 4 March those fingers!

4 Are your fingertips tip-top? Check for a rounded hand shape. Try playing with a duet. Say finger numbers four times with gusto!

(See Video and Duet Appendix p. 140)

explore & create

- **Flipping Flashcards**
  Play one pattern four times, then I'll point to the next while you're on the fourth turn. Change to the new one without missing a beat!

- **Flashcard Whiz**
  Play one pattern twice, then I'll point to the next. Keep the beat! Keep saying the numbers!

- **Flashcard Daredevil**
  Play a pattern once, then I'll point to the next. Both hands ready. Here we go!

- **Flashcard Magician**
  Play matching flashcards hands together! (mirror image)

- **Flashcard Olympics**
  No hopping off the finger.
  Stay on the mat!
  Firm fingertips rate a high score!
  Can you get a Perfect Ten?

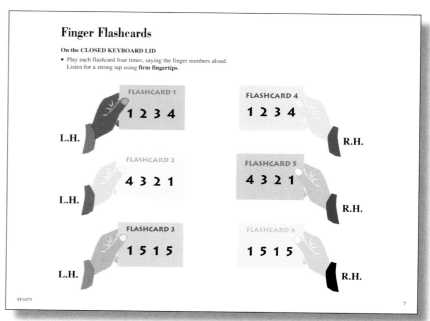

Finger Flashcards

On the CLOSED KEYBOARD LID

- Play each flashcard four times, saying the finger numbers aloud. Listen for a strong tap using **firm fingertips**.

FLASHCARD 1   1 2 3 4   L.H.

FLASHCARD 4   1 2 3 4   R.H.

FLASHCARD 2   4 3 2 1   L.H.

FLASHCARD 5   4 3 2 1   R.H.

FLASHCARD 3   1 5 1 5   L.H.

FLASHCARD 6   1 5 1 5   R.H.

FF1075

7

pedagogy pointers

Knowing finger numbers is the first step in getting fingers to move in succession.

Fingering is often a matter of using established patterns, so it's useful to prepare the student to think in that way, and to experience these patterns in the hand before needing to play them on the keyboard.

For most young students, finger independence develops only gradually because it requires finer control of small muscles and joints.

Finger "warm-ups" get fingers ready for what's to come.

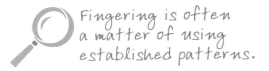

Fingering is often a matter of using established patterns.

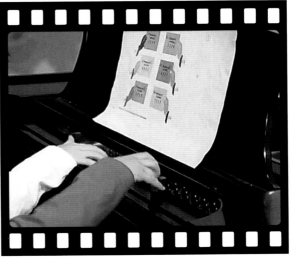

PIANO ADVENTURES VIDEO

see it in action

Teaching Video 4

We're off to the Piano Olympics Finger Gymnastics! And these are definitely some winning teams. The energy is high, the fingers are ready to whip through the drills, and finger numbers ring out with cheer-leading enthusiasm. The strategy is to balance on the starting finger, then keep your fingers "on the mat" as each flashcard gets the Royal Four treatment.

Sometimes the fingers strut in succession, sometimes they rock from side to side. The drills can be done with or without a music accompaniment. The excitement builds as the speed increases, and goes over the top as the hands play together. Bring out the gold medals. We've got Perfect Tens!

Ask Yourself

■ Can you think of other finger patterns that would make good flashcards?

■ What is the value of a musical accompaniment to finger drills like these?

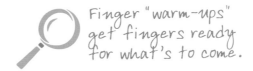

Finger "warm-ups" get fingers ready for what's to come.

The Pecking Rooster/Hen

Lesson Book pages 8-9

INTRODUCTION

what's new

- **Up the keyboard = right/high Down the keyboard = left/low**
- **Braced finger**

what's important

- **Firm fingertip and rounded hand shape**
- **Playing down/up entire keyboard**
- **"Pecking" with a sticky staccato and a flexible wrist**

let's get started

1 Let's make a rooster peck for seeds going down the keyboard. We'll go low—to the left, with your left hand.

2 (Show braced 3rd finger) Look at my hand. The rooster pecks right on the tip, his beak.

3 When your rooster pecks down (lower), lean your body to the left.

4 Your rooster shouldn't have a stiff neck. Keep your wrist loose!

5 Your right hand is a little hen. She pecks up (higher) on the keyboard. Lean your body to the right. Keep your wrist loose!

explore & create

- **The Hen's Duet** The hen can peck up the keys quickly. (Play a quick accompaniment.)

- **The Rooster's Duet** The rooster struts around in the dark. (Play a slow, mysterious accompaniment.)

- **Rooster and Hen Together** Use two hands. The rooster (LH) pecks in place on Middle C as the hen (RH) pecks up the white keys. Hands alternate as they play. Reverse.

(See Video)

Remember— you're the model!

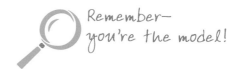

Practice Steps

1. On the closed keyboard lid, your teacher will tap a steady beat. Match the beat with your **left hand.**

2. Now set a steady "L.H. beat" for your teacher to match!

3. To play, start in the **middle** of the piano. Brace your 3rd finger with the thumb and "peck" all the white keys going LOWER—to the left.

This is going **DOWN** the keyboard.

The Pecking Rooster
FOR LEFT HAND ON WHITE KEYS

L.H.

DOWN
When the keys are lower, the sound is lower!
Keep a great steady beat!

LOW ... MIDDLE C

Teacher Duet: (Student begins on Middle C and plays a quarter-note beat going lower.)

8ᵛᵃ throughout

8   5

FF1075

partner pages

Technique & Artistry
p. 5 Making O's

■ See Teacher Manual p. 13. Encourage students to notice that Making O's is at work for The Pecking Rooster/Hen!

pedagogy pointers

Establishing a natural, curved, flexible hand position is the basis of keyboard technique. Playing with a braced third finger is an effective approach. Both arch and fingertip are supported. Using a non-legato touch (like a sticky staccato) at the beginning helps direct the arm weight from the shoulder.

The left hand can be the first to try out the new technique. It won't play "second fiddle" to the right hand, which often gets the most attention. The student begins to associate "down" with going to the left and making low sounds. The right hand will then go "up" to make high sounds.

As the student moves from key to key with a braced third finger, guide the student to develop a flexible wrist. Your own example should be the ideal model. You may need to help some students with this technique—either by placing a finger under the wrist so the hand falls from the wrist, or by suggesting that the finger springs off the key like a trampoline.

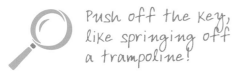

Push off the key, like springing off a trampoline!

PIANO ADVENTURES VIDEO

see it in action

Teaching Video 5

The Pecking Rooster and Hen explore the entire keyboard range, at the same time teaching higher, up, and to the right (and then reverse). Olivia's hen and rooster release each "peck", and her wrists are loose and flexible—no stiff "necks".

Different accompaniments encourage steady rhythm within a musical context.

"Pecking" with alternating hands helps Vivian achieve a natural body balance. This is one musical barnyard!

Ask Yourself

■ Why is it important to lean in the direction the hand is moving?

■ How would you describe the teacher's involvement as the student plays?

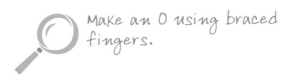

Make an O using braced fingers.

Two Black Ants

Lesson Book page 10

what's new

- 2-black-key groups
- 3-black-key groups

what's important

- Finding 2-black-key groups
- Using LH fingers 2 and 3
- Playing a piece in the lower range of the keyboard

let's get started

1 (Show how the black keys are divided into groups of 2s and 3s.)

2 Put your LH fingertips together, like a bubble. Touch all the 2-black-keys starting in the middle and going lower.

3 Let's watch those ants march down the page. Take this pencil in your LH and point while I play.

4 Use just two fingers—LH 2 and 3. (Demonstrate playing 2-3-together on the music rack or fallboard.)

5 Let's play this pattern on each group of 2-black-keys going down the keyboard. (Begin in the middle)

explore & create

- **Crawling Up**
  The ants might also crawl up the keyboard. Start at the bottom and play 2-3-together up to the middle.

- **Ear Tunes!**
  Keep fingers 2 and 3 over the 2-black-keys. Close your eyes! I'll play a little pattern. You play it back!

- **Test the Teacher!**
  I'll close my eyes and you make up patterns for me to repeat.

- **Composing!**
  Make up your own short pattern for fingers 2 and 3 on the 2-black-keys. Play this pattern from the middle going down the keyboard. You just composed a piece!

 Guide the student to read patterns, not individual notes or fingers.

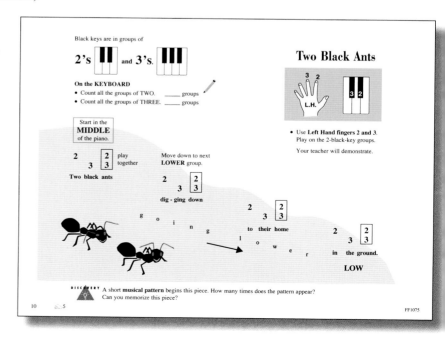

partner pages

Technique & Artistry
pp. 4-5 Five Secrets for Piano Technique

- Two Black Ants uses Technique Secrets 1-3: Karate Pose, Blooming Flowers, and Making O's.

- All students should be able to maintain good posture and a rounded hand shape. Many students, however, will find keeping firm fingertips a challenge.

- Realize this is a first piece and that it is an ongoing skill to develop firm fingertips.

- Because ants are very quiet creatures, the student may play softly which can help prevent the fingertip from collapsing.

- Some students may enjoy making a round "ant hill shape" as they move to each lower black-key-group. This image will help them use relaxed arm movements.

pedagogy pointers

We find our way around the keyboard by means of the black keys. So learning those groups of two and three keys is a natural introduction to piano "geography". At the same time, the student is introduced to off-staff notation and directional reading. The fingering groups move down the page, and going to the left on the keyboard is associated with lower sounds. Since the left hand often gets less attention, it gets the first chance to play a piece.

Using off-staff notation (pre-reading), a student can begin to see that music is made up of patterns—note or melody patterns, fingering patterns, rhythm patterns, and aural patterns. That is the best way to learn to read—in groups, rather than note-by-note.

 Creating an original pattern is evidence that a student understands what a pattern is.

PIANO ADVENTURES VIDEO

see it in action

Teaching Video 6

The off-staff notation gives a clear picture of where to look and Olivia points the way while she listens. Warming up the 2-3-together pattern before trying it out on the 2-black-key groups gets her ready to play from the middle to the bottom.

That was so easy, she learns a new pattern. Better still, Olivia creates one of her own.

Then she discovers that she can play back music messages, even with her eyes closed. Those two left-hand fingers can do amazing things!

Ask Yourself

- When the teacher says, "Scoot back, Olivia", what does Olivia do?

- What else do the play-back messages support besides hearing tonal direction?

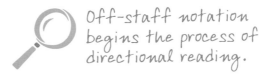 Off-staff notation begins the process of directional reading.

UNIT 1

INTRODUCTION

Two Blackbirds

Lesson Book page 11

what's new

- **Playing 2-black-key groups in the higher keyboard range**

what's important

- **Using RH fingers 2 and 3**
- **Going up the keyboard = playing higher**
- **The hand should float from group to group, flexing at the wrist**

let's get started

1 Put your RH fingertips together, like a bubble. Touch all the 2-black-keys starting in the middle and going higher.

2 These two blackbirds are going to fly up the keyboard, moving higher to the sky.

3 Use RH fingers 2-3. (Try 2-3-together on the music rack or fallboard.)

4 Let's play this pattern on each group of 2-black-keys going up the keyboard. (Begin in the middle)

5 Make sure your hand floats up to the next group of 2-black-keys.

A creative change can transform drill into a musical experience.

explore & create

- **Flying Down**
  The birds could fly down the keyboard. Start at the top and play RH fingers 2-3-together down to the middle.

- **Ear Tunes!**
  Keep fingers 2 and 3 over the 2-black-keys. Close your eyes! I'll play a little pattern. You play it back!

- **Test the Teacher!**
  I'll close my eyes and you make up patterns for me to repeat.

- **Transposing!**
  Turn the two blackbirds into two snowflakes. Slide RH fingers 2-3 down to the two white keys (C and D). Try it with a duet.

  (Duet Appendix p. 140)

- **Improvising!**
  Create a swirling snow storm. You play any high white keys with my duet.

  (See Video and Duet Appendix pp. 140-141)

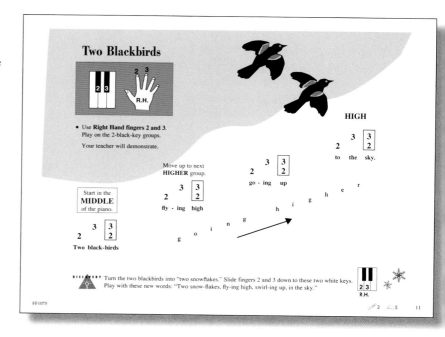

20

partner pages

Theory
p. 3 Low and High Sounds

■ Ants marching lower and blackbirds flying higher guide shading the 2 and 3-black-key groups—low to high and high to low. Next, students shade a white key lower or higher from the ant or blackbird.

Technique & Artistry
pp. 4-5 Five Secrets for Piano Technique

■ Two Blackbirds also uses Technique Secrets 1-3: Karate Pose, Blooming Flowers, and Making O's.

■ Students can begin to explore graceful arm movement as the RH gently flies to higher black-key-groups.

■ A bird doesn't fly sideways—it flies up and then down to land gently. Demonstrate a gentle arc and ask the student to copy.

■ Some students will also find this challenging. Touch lightly on it as an introduction. There will be many opportunities to explore graceful arm motion.

pedagogy pointers

Now the right hand gets a chance to play a piece that moves up the keyboard. Similar off-staff notation shows directional reading that moves up the page. The fingering and rhythm patterns are the same as in the previous piece, making it easy for the student to focus on the single new concept—up the keyboard.

Take the necessary time to establish an easy wrist-arm-shoulder connection right at the start because it's the key to a fluid technique. Some children do this naturally. Others need specific physical guidance and time to judge for themselves whether they are moving gracefully from octave to octave.

PIANO ADVENTURES VIDEO

see it in action

Teaching Video 7

These birds visit the 2-black-key groups going up the keyboard. The birds also need to learn to fly gracefully from group to group. The trick is to have a loose wrist that lifts the hand and arm to the next octave. With a magic "whoosh" Patrick sees these birds turn into snowflakes! The experience moving up the keyboard is the same, but the mood has changed. And a lovely original snowfall is the musical finish to what began as a technical workout. Magic, indeed!

(Duet Appendix pp. 140-141)

Ask Yourself

■ When the teacher first demonstrates the piece, where are Patrick's eyes?

■ When Patrick first plays the piece by memory, what does the teacher add? What is the effect?

■ How does the teacher support Patrick's several attempts to "fly" up the keyboard?

The student needs to internalize the feel of the physical gesture.

Into the Cave

Lesson Book page 12

what's new

- Playing 3-black-key groups in the lower keyboard range

what's important

- Finding 3-black-key groups
- Using LH fingers 2-3-4
- The hand should float from group to group, flexing at the wrist

let's get started

1 If you were going into a cave, would you be going higher or lower?

2 Let's touch all the 3-black-keys. Start in the middle and go lower.

3 As the boys explore the cave, let's explore the music on the page. You point to the finger numbers as I play.

4 Fingers 2-3-4 will walk down, then stop and listen when the fingers play together. (Demonstrate)

5 Are you ready to explore the cave? Make sure your hand floats down to the next group of 3-black-keys.

Using the middle fingers helps to center the hand.

explore & create

- **Bold Explorers!**
  Let's explore sound. These boys are brave and stomp down into the dark cave loudly.

- **Scaredy Cats!**
  It can be spooky in the cave. These explorers tiptoe slowly and softly. Watch out for bats!

- **Ear Tunes!**
  Keep LH fingers 2-3-4 over the 3-black-keys. Close your eyes! I'll play a little pattern. You play it back!

- **Batty Duet!**
  Show another student how to play this 2-black-key rhythm high on the keyboard. Use the words: *Lit-tle bat.*
  Play a duet with two students.

(See Video)

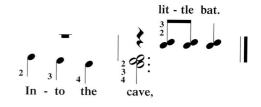

Into the Cave

L.H.

- Use **Left Hand fingers 2, 3, and 4.** Play on the 3-black-key groups.

  Your teacher will demonstrate.

Start in the **MIDDLE** of the piano.

2 3 4 | 2 3 4 play together

In - to the cave,

Move down to next **LOWER** group.

2 3 4 | 2 3 4

if you are brave,

2 3 4 | 2 3 4

deep down and low!
LOW

DISCOVERY Point out the **musical pattern** used in this piece. How many times does it appear? _____

12 4-5 5 2

FF1075

partner pages

Theory
pp. 4-5 Into the Cave Improvisation

■ Students learn the word improvisation and create "into the cave" music with a teacher duet—all on the black keys. The range of the keyboard is explored from high to low as student and teacher descend deep down into the cave!

Technique & Artistry
pp. 4-5 Five Secrets for Piano Technique

■ As students play fingers 2-3-4 together on the 3-black-keys, individual fingers may tend to flatten.

■ If this happens, coach the student to roll the flattened fingers forward to a rounded hand shape.

■ For Into the Cave, play and say aloud, "2-3-4 together, ROLL UP" or "2-3-4 together, ROLL OFF"

   The held black-key cluster gives a great opportunity to check and re-balance on the fingertips.

pedagogy pointers

Once again, the left hand is the first to investigate more of the keyboard, this time the 3-black-key groups. Using the middle fingers keeps the hand in a natural position and directs the weight to the center of the hand. Playing from the middle to the bottom of the keyboard reinforces moving "down" the keyboard.

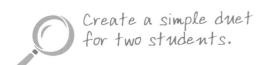

Create a simple duet for two students.

PIANO ADVENTURES VIDEO

see it in action

Teaching Video 8

Exploring a cave can be scary, but not if you do it with friends. The middle fingers of the left hand go down, down, down—but stop at each level to check around them. Olivia sees that the notes on the page also march down into the ground. Deep, down, and low certainly sounds spooky, especially when the explorers tiptoe to the bottom.

Those bats that hang from the ceiling of the cave have a chance to flutter their wings as part of an easy duet that can be done with a friend. Vivian's "lit-tle bat" creates more mystery while Olivia bravely finishes with two hands way down low. Who's got the flashlight?

Ask Yourself

■ What changes in Olivia's gestures when the "boys tiptoe down into the cave"?

■ Besides mystery, what does Vivian's duet add to the performance?

Three Little Kittens

Lesson Book page 13

what's new

- Playing 3-black-key groups in the higher range of the keyboard

what's important

- Finding 3-black-key groups
- Using RH fingers 2-3-4
- The hand should float from group to group, flexing at the wrist

let's get started

1 Let's touch all the 3-black-keys. Start in the middle and go higher.

2 Stay on the highest 3-black-key group. At the end of this piece, these three kittens are going to meow together. Let's try it out.

3 Here's our finger trick! Try 2-3-4 together on the fallboard.

4 Let's play that pattern finding each group of 3-black-keys going up the keyboard. (Begin in the middle)

5 Make sure your hand floats up to the next group of 3-black-keys.

6 Spring off for the last meow!

explore & create

- **How Old Are You?**
  Would you meow that many times when you get to the end?

- **Ear Tunes!**
  Keep fingers 2-3-4 over the 3-black-keys. Close your eyes! I'll play a little pattern using these fingers and keys. Can you play it back?

- **Play with a Friend!**
  (Have a slightly older student play F-sharp with the LH and the 2-black-keys with the RH in 3/4.) Left-right-right, Left-right-right … soft paws!

  (See Video and Duet Appendix p. 142)

- **Composing!**
  Make up your own pattern for fingers 2-3-4 on the 3-black-keys. Play this pattern from the middle going up the keyboard. Another composition!

A moderate tempo gives time to move gracefully to the next octave.

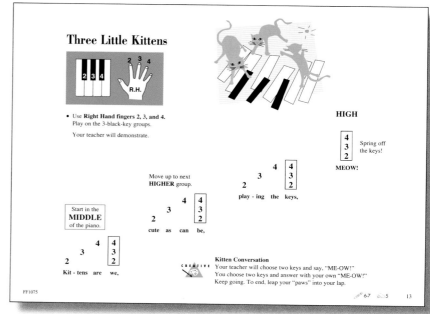

partner pages

Theory

Eye-Training and Ear-Training are presented as two distinct activities featured regularly in the Piano Adventures method.

p. 6 Inspect the Notes!

■ For Eye-Training, students explore the direction of the notes by circling going UP, going DOWN, or going UP and DOWN to match the "round noteheads".

p. 7 Be All Ears!

■ For Ear-Training, students listen and circle if the sounds are going higher or lower. Can your students make up their own "going higher" and "going lower" examples?

Technique & Artistry
pp. 4-5 Five Secrets for Piano Technique

■ Encourage students to spring off the highest "meow" for Three Little Kittens and drop into the lap with arm weight. The cat has landed!

Performance
p. 2 In the Jungle

■ Have the student play slowly on the lowest 3-black-key groups. Tell the student you're an elephant doctor and will be studying the elephant legs (fingers) very closely. Move low and close to the student's fingers. This scrutiny will focus attention on firm fingertips.

pedagogy pointers

A piece on 3-black-keys for the right hand completes the exploration of the black-key groupings over the entire range of the keyboard. It also reinforces moving "up" the keyboard.

Ending a piece played with a partner is just as important as beginning together.

PIANO ADVENTURES VIDEO

see it in action

Teaching Video 9

Three little kittens may have lost their mittens but they know how to find the 3-black-key groups that go to the top of the keyboard. How quickly Olivia catches on to the pattern, even before the demonstration is over. No wonder there's a secret smile.

Each time the kittens spring to the next group is a chance to use a floating wrist. And the last "meow" is the really big "spring". How nice to have a friend who can join you by providing a "Kit-ty Cat" accompaniment, like kittens walking on little, soft paws. After a trial run, let's make it a recital, complete with a well-deserved bow. Who needs teachers?

Ask Yourself

■ What is the purpose of those first seven springy meows?

■ Compare Olivia's final performances of Into the Cave and Three Little Kittens. What has improved?

Pulse Is What "Counts"

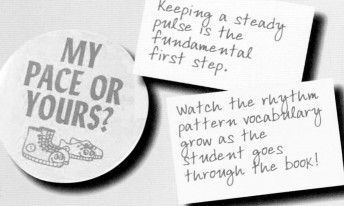

"Rhythm" comes from the Greek word for "measured flow".

Pulse (Flow)

- Keeping a steady pulse is the fundamental first step
- May be slow or fast, but it must be steady
- Should be experienced before it's associated with ♩
- Chant 1-1-1-1 or ta-ta-ta-ta or walk-walk-walk-walk

Meter (Measure)

- Organizes pulses in a recurring accented group
- Each meter implies certain accents and non-accents
- 4/4 and 3/4 are the meters taught at the Primer Level

Feel! Flow! Fun!

- Playing with and for the student develops a "feel" for rhythms.
- Encourage the student to express pulse and rhythm with large, as well as smaller, motions.
- The student should hear and play meters and rhythms without needing to "know about" them.

Rhythm

- Is a pattern of short and long sounds
- Rhythm patterns don't exist until you introduce the ♩
- A rhythm pattern is a short group of notes
- Rhythm patterns should be felt as a group

Tempo

- Is the speed at which the pulses occur
- Playing in many different tempos should be encouraged
- Tempos usually imply moods or feelings

MY PACE OR YOURS?

Keeping a steady pulse is the fundamental first step.

Watch the rhythm pattern vocabulary grow as the student goes through the book!

Count: 1   1   1 - 2

Teach rhythm patterns ...

■ Each rhythm pattern is a *group* of notes that should be seen and learned as a *unit*.

■ Usual patterns such as these recur throughout the Primer Level books:

■ Reading patterns as groups instills the feeling for the natural accents/non-accents characteristic of each group.

... but count note values

At this early level, encourage the student to count the note *values* aloud. For example, a quarter note is counted as "1", and a half note as "1-2" regardless of position in the measure.

This "unit counting" reinforces the meaning of the note values and does not overwhelm the student with the difficulties of counting the meter aloud while playing (e.g., 1-2-3-4 for every measure).

Yet we still teach meter by counting the time signature while the student plays, by asking the student to count the time signature while the teacher plays, and with written work in the Theory Book and on a white board.

Flow over the bar line

■ The student should play at many tempos, including fast tempos.

■ Playing in quick tempos teaches the student to read, think, and play *over the bar line*.

■ A flow over the bar line improves musicality by conveying the expressive character of meter.

To promote fluent playing and the musicality of meter, eighth notes are not introduced until Level 2A of Piano Adventures.

Thus, you can encourage faster tempos as the student improves on a piece. Some pieces may even take the feel of cut time.

The student should play at many tem-pos.

Every student wants to play fast. Playing fast is energizing, exciting, and expressive!

Group lesson—3:30pm

The Quarter Note

Lesson Book page 14

what's new

■ Steady pulse

■ Quarter note

what's important

■ Feeling and keeping a steady pulse

■ Recognizing the quarter note
  How it feels
  How it sounds
  How it looks

let's get started

1 Music must have a steady beat. The beat can be fast or slow, but it must be steady.

2 (Get a steady beat going. Clap, tap, march, or use a drum.)

3 Can you keep a steady beat with me? Let's count "1" (or "ta" or "walk") for each beat.

4 A quarter note can be a picture for one beat. It's got a head and a stem, and it's all colored in. Let's sing together!

(See Video and Duet Appendix p. 143)

explore & create

■ **Fast and Slow Steady Beat**
I'll play two examples of a steady beat. Tell me which is fast, which is slow.

■ **Listen to My Beats**
Raise your hand when you hear the beat getting faster or slower.

■ **Metronome Fun**
Listen to this! (Use a metronome.) Beats can be very slow, or very fast. Choose keys to play with braced finger 3s and match the beat.

■ **Haydn Concerto**
I'm going to play some fast, fancy music. You play steady quarter notes and help me feel the beat!

(See Video and Duet Appendix pp. 144-145)

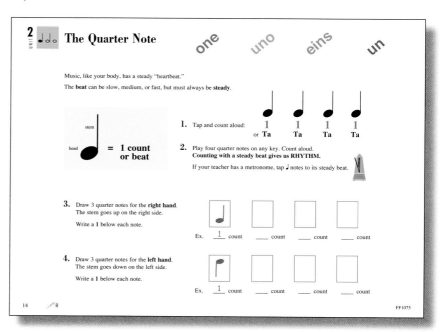

♪ ♫ Duet Appendix pp. 143-145

partner pages

Theory
p. 8 The Quarter Note

Guide the student through the activities on the page. More activities might include:

- Make a ♩ note out of clay

- Find hidden ♩ notes in the studio

- Writes his or her age in ♩ notes

  (7 years = ♩ ♩ ♩ ♩ ♩ ♩ ♩)

pedagogy pointers

Keeping a steady pulse is fundamental to good musicianship—at all levels, and at all times. At the beginning, therefore, it's important that the concept of pulse is internalized. All rhythm patterns build on that single principle.

Pulse must become a kinesthetic experience, something felt internally. Using different physical gestures—like tapping, walking, clapping, or drumming—to establish a sense of pulse is more important than "counting".

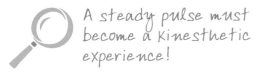
A steady pulse must become a kinesthetic experience!

PIANO ADVENTURES VIDEO

see it in action

Teaching Video 10

Although it's necessary to "see" how quarter notes look, and to "know" that each quarter note gets one count, feeling a steady pulse is the heart of the matter. A little song guides Olivia to draw notes and add stems. But playing quarter notes within a musical context is the real achievement. Olivia is taking those first, big steady steps!

Ask Yourself

- How does the teacher handle Olivia's rushing notes when Olivia first begins to play as part of the "duet"?

- What are some differences between Olivia's right and left-hand "duet" performances?

BASIC RHYTHMS

The Old Clock

Lesson Book page 15

- **Keeping a steady beat**
- **Playing with alternating hands**

what's important

- **Feeling a steady beat in the body**
- **Dropping arm weight from the shoulders**

let's get started

1 Let's pretend we're clocks. (Combine saying Tick-Tock with swaying from side to side, like a pendulum.)

2 What's the most important thing about a clock? (Answer: it must keep steady time.)

3 This time both hands are going to play. Let's see how. (Have student point to the notes as you play the piece.)

4 (Tap the piece, using the hands as written. First say right-left, etc., then the words.) Is your clock steady?

5 Let's put our clock on the 2-black-key groups and listen to it keep steady time. (Play the piece.)

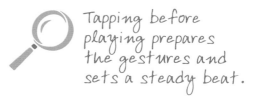

Tapping before playing prepares the gestures and sets a steady beat.

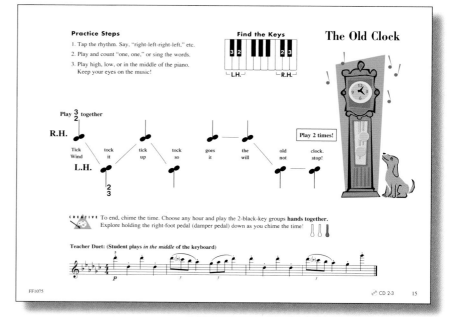

Practice Steps

1. Tap the rhythm. Say, "right-left-right-left," etc.
2. Play and count "one, one," or sing the words.
3. Play high, low, or in the middle of the piano. Keep your eyes on the music!

Find the Keys

The Old Clock

Play **3/2** together

R.H.

Tick tock tick tock goes the old clock.
Wind it up so it will not stop!

L.H.

Play 2 times!

CREATIVE To end, chime the time. Choose any hour and play the 2-black-key groups **hands together.** Explore holding the right-foot pedal (damper pedal) down as you chime the time!

Teacher Duet: (Student plays *in the middle* of the keyboard)

FF1075   CD 2-3   15

explore & create

- **A Big Grandfather Clock**
(Play the piece low on the keyboard. Slow and steady.)

- **A Tiny Table Clock or Wrist Watch**
(Play the piece high on the keyboard, quicker and softer.)

- **Ring Those Chimes!**
Create some long, loud chimes—play groups of 2-black-keys with both hands. Then, still on the 2-black-keys, create short chime sounds. Alternate hands and play quicker and softer. Let's improvise a duet together.

(See Video and Duet Appendix pp. 146-147)

pedagogy pointers

This is the first piece that uses both hands. Playing with regularly alternating hands develops upper body balance and reinforces gestures made with the entire arm, dropping from the shoulders.

The finger clusters never change notes, so the student can focus attention on the alternating hand motions. The eyes learn to track from left to right and up and down—a development of directional reading.

Large body gestures help internalize the beat.

Playing with alternating hands keeps the body in balance.

PIANO ADVENTURES VIDEO

see it in action

Teaching Video 11

Tapping before playing prepares the gestures and sets a steady beat. Kai feels the beat with her whole arm and upper torso as she plays. And playing the duet proves that she can keep a steady beat.

This clock has chimes that can ring louder and longer and smaller chimes that ring more quickly and softly. As part of an improvised duet, Kai continues to develop a sense of steady beat in a musical context—right to the stroke of midnight!

Ask Yourself

- Can you think of other movements that might imitate "ticks"?

- How does the teacher prepare the chime and gong improvisation?

The Walking Song

Lesson Book page 16

what's new

- **Playing with fingers 2-3-4 in stepwise motion, down and up**
- **Double bar line**

what's important

- **Playing with fingers 2-3-4 on 3-black-keys in stepwise motion (non-legato is acceptable at this stage)**
- **Keeping a steady beat**

let's get started

1 Let's take a short walk in the studio. Step, step, step, step ... you keep a steady beat, don't you?

2 Imitate me. Let's walk fingers 2-3-4 up and down on the 3-black-keys. Are you steady?

3 Point to the notes while I play The Walking Song. Watch the notes move up and down. Which note repeats?

4 (On the fallboard) Play and say the finger numbers.

5 (On the keys) Play and say the finger numbers. Is your walk steady?

explore & create

- **Is That an Elephant Walking?**
  (Play the piece slow, heavy, and low on the keyboard.)

- **How Would a Pony Trot?**
  (Play the piece in the middle range, lighter and quicker.)

- **Can You Sneak in on Tiptoe?**
  (Play the piece high on the keyboard, very soft and very light.)

- **Here Comes a King!**
  (Play with a stately and solemn quarter-note accompaniment. Student plays 1 octave higher.)

  (See Video and Duet Appendix p. 148)

- **Be a Clown**
  (Play a quirky eighth-note accompaniment. Student plays 1 octave higher.)

  (See Video and Duet Appendix p. 148)

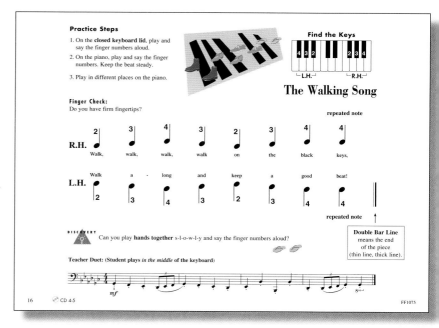

♪♫ Duet Appendix pp. 148-149

CD Tracks 4-5
8-measure IMPROVISATION at the end.
Students may freely play any black keys.

■ **Swing Time**
(Play an accompaniment with triplets. Student plays 1 octave lower.)

(See Video and Duet Appendix p. 149)

■ **Tooth Fairy**
Does the tooth fairy still visit? (Play an accompaniment with sixteenths. Student plays as written.)

(See Video and Duet Appendix p. 149)

pedagogy pointers

Now it's time for the fingers to move individually. Staying on the 3-black-keys and using fingers 2-3-4 keeps the hand in balance as each finger steps up and down. The left hand first walks down, then up because that's the most natural gesture.

At this stage playing legato is not yet the ideal. The movement of the notes on the page is more subtle, and the repeated note is introduced.

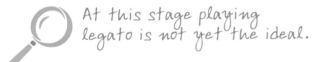

At this stage playing legato is not yet the ideal.

PIANO ADVENTURES VIDEO

see it in action

Teaching Video 12

Patrick knows that walking must be steady, otherwise the motion would be jerky. But there are so many ways to walk! A king would strut, a clown might prance, you could sway from side to side, or even sneak into the room! Patrick tries them all and reacts accordingly as he becomes part of a larger musical context. Who knew repetition could be so exciting!

Ask Yourself

■ What was Patrick's special "clown" ending?

■ What does the teacher do to create and guide the various improvisations?

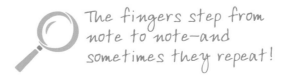

The fingers step from note to note—and sometimes they repeat!

Tightrope Walker

Lesson Book page 17

what's new

- Many repeated notes
- Coordinated use of fingers 2-3-4

what's important

- Feeling the keys
- Balancing close to the keys when playing repeated notes
- Playing steady quarter notes when playing repeated notes

let's get started

1 Suppose you were a tightrope walker. In order to walk across the wire, would you jump, or stay close to the wire?

2 Place fingers 2-3-4 over the 3-black-keys. Let's try repeating finger 2 (or 3 or 4, either hand) without falling off the key.

3 Let's check the piece. Which hand and finger has the most repeated notes? Can you play these and stay balanced?

4 Get ready to play the piece. Balance by staying close to the key and feeling your fingertips. Don't hop too high!

explore & create

- **Play It Safe**
  Let's be cautious and put the tightrope wire close to the ground. (Play low.)

- **How Daring Are You?**
  (Play the piece higher and higher on the keyboard. Provide a simple duet.)

- **No Eyes on the Music**
  Can you play the piece without looking at the music? Choose where you'd like to put your tightrope wire.

- **Duet on the Tightrope**
  Sometimes tightrope walkers work with a partner. (Show another student how to play an easy duet: F-sharp [LH] C-sharp [RH], alternating in steady quarter notes.) Keep that wire steady. Fingers close to the keys! (See Video)

- **Transposition**
  What if you hopped down to the white keys (G-A-B)?

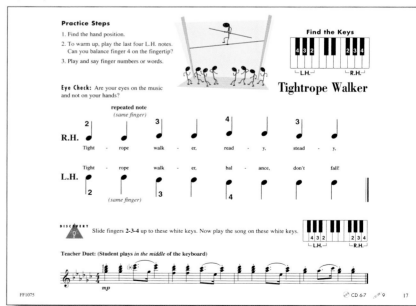

Stay close to the key when playing repeat-ed notes!

34

partner pages

Theory
p. 9 Your High-Wire Tune

- For Eye-Training, students create a first composition using only quarter notes. Students choose finger numbers 2, 3, or 4 to create a simple three-note melody.

- Then for Ear-Training, students explore playing the new tune with two contrasting teacher duets; one calm and one quirky. Listen for which is which!

pedagogy pointers

The emphasis here is on reading and playing repeated notes. On the page, the finger number for the repeated note is omitted, encouraging the student to recognize the repetition and the horizontal movement of the notes.

The technique trick is to stay close to the key when playing the repeated note. Comparison to the movements of a tightrope walker is a vivid teaching strategy.

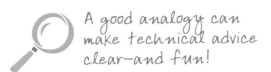

A good analogy can make technical advice clear—and fun!

PIANO ADVENTURES VIDEO

see it in action

Teaching Video 13

Playing repeated notes can sometimes be dangerous! If you pop up too high, you might lose your balance and fall off those black keys. Stay close to the keys as you move from note to note.

Kai and Vivian start their tightrope walk by testing how to balance on their LH fourth fingers, the finger that has the most repeated notes. They even check their sitting distance by doing the "karate pose".

Sometimes a tightrope walker works with a partner. The partner also has to keep a good balance. These experts are ready for the Big Top!

Ask Yourself

- What is the key word guiding the technical approach?

- Could you suggest a further step to improve the duet performance?

The Half Note

Lesson Book page 18

what's new

- **The Half Note**

what's important

- **Feeling half notes**
- **Recognizing half notes**
- **Understanding the relationship between half and quarter notes**

let's get started

1 Let's walk across the studio in slow steps. (Count 1-2, 1-2 as you walk.) Now let's cross the studio quickly. (Count 1, 1, 1, 1 …)

2 I'll take a walk. Am I walking in half or quarter notes? (Demonstrate. Bend at the knees to pulse the half notes.)

3 (Use the book to show how half notes look.)

4 Let's draw some half notes. Use the book and the chant: "It's got a head and a stem, but it's not colored in."

(Duet Appendix p. 150)

5 Choose any key(s). Use one hand, or both. (Guide the student to play half notes, then quarter notes. Switch back and forth.)

explore & create

■ **Step on it!**
Sit forward on a bench or chair so that the feet touch the floor. "Step" from one foot to the other, counting 1, 1, 1, 1.

At the same time clap, counting 1, 1, 1, 1 (quarter notes). Then clap half notes, counting 1-2, 1-2. The feet continue to step in quarter notes. Switch back and forth.

■ **Love that Beat!**
Have the student play half and quarter note Gs high on the keyboard while you play a short piece of music. March music is effective for this.

(See Video of Bach's Musette in G and Duet Appendix p. 151)

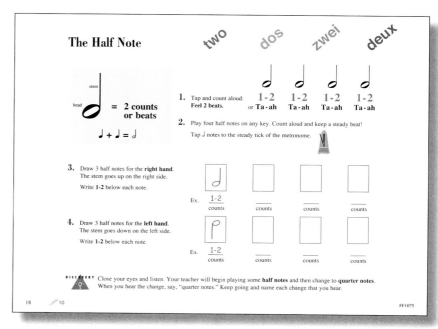

♪♫ Duet Appendix pp. 150-151

partner pages

Theory
p. 10 The Half Note

Guide the student through the activities on the page. Additional activities might include:

- Make a ♩ out of clay
- Finds hidden ♩ and ♩ notes in the studio
- Write his/her age in ♩ notes and ♩ notes

pedagogy pointers

The most important thing about rhythm is that it must be felt. Keeping a steady beat must be established in order to feel notes that are twice as long as the beat itself. It's a matter of kinesthetics, not mathematics.

Kinesthetics describes the awareness you have of motion, especially the motion, balance, position, and weight of your own body.

Helping a student achieve that awareness is at the heart of teaching rhythm.

 *Rhythm is an inner awareness, not a counting system.*

PIANO ADVENTURES VIDEO

see it in action

Teaching Video 14

Drawing half notes helps Patrick see how half notes look. A new version of the song reminds him that half notes are "not colored in".

It's a lot of fun to play and feel rhythms together, making music with friends. Kai and Vivian switch between half and quarter notes with braced fingers and flexible wrists. And how musical it all becomes when they make a rhythm ensemble to Bach's Musette. Bagpipes are in the air!

Ask Yourself

- What other motions or activities could you use to help a student feel the difference between half notes and quarter notes?
- How can you tell that Kai and Vivian feel the beat and note values?

 Changing note values as part of a duet is a musical experience.

The I Like Song

Lesson Book page 19

what's new

- Playing half notes in a piece

what's important

- Feeling the difference between quarter notes and half notes

- Recognizing and feeling the half note as part of a rhythm pattern (♩ ♩ 𝅗𝅥)

let's get started

1 Here's a rhythm pattern that uses the half note. (Demonstrate ♩ ♩ 𝅗𝅥) This is how it looks. (Show the pattern in the piece.)

2 Let's tap and count the rhythm in this piece. Tap with the hand that plays and count 1, 1, 1-2.

3 Be a rhythm detective. Find and circle that pattern in the piece.

4 Find the 3-black-keys in both hands with fingers 2-3-4. We'll play and say the finger numbers.

5 Now let's play the piece and count 1, 1, 1-2.

Look for patterns. Don't read note to note!

explore & create

- **Mystery Position**
(Student's fingers should be on the 3-black-keys.) Close your eyes. I'm going to move your fingers to a mystery position. (Slide them down to F-G-A high on the keyboard.)
Let's play with a bluesy duet.

(Duet Appendix p. 152)

- **Spooky Position**
I'm going to move your fingers to a spooky position! (Slide fingers over A-B-C high on the keyboard.) Let's pretend it's Halloween and change the words, too. (Play and sing with a spooky duet.)

(Duet Appendix p. 152)

- **Tooth Fairy Position**
(Place the student's hands on G-A-B high on the keyboard.) This fairy is coming in on tiptoe so she doesn't wake anybody. (Play a music-box duet.)

(Duet Appendix p. 153)

BASIC RHYTHMS

♪♫ Duet Appendix pp. 152-153

CD Tracks 8-9
8-measure IMPROVISATION at the end.
Students may freely play any black keys.

partner pages

Technique & Artistry
pp. 6-7 Firming Up My Fingers

■ In the Technique & Artistry books, one of the five Technique Secrets serves as a warm-up and guide for each exercise that follows.

■ Firm fingertips (Making O's) is at the root of Firming Up My Fingers, a hands alone, black-key exercise using fingers 2-3-4. Repeated notes are a key element here. A firm fingertip is developed as each finger in turn plays the six-note rhythm pattern.

Performance
p. 3 The Doorbell

■ The Doorbell isolates fingers 2 and 4. Many students need reinforcement for these fingers.

■ The half-note opening allows the hand to balance and prepare for the next note.

■ Encourage students to find and circle this rhythm pattern for each hand:

♩ ♩ ♩ ♩ ♩   ♩

pedagogy pointers

The first piece that uses half notes, The I Like Song, also establishes a new rhythm pattern. It's important that note values are not seen as isolated elements, but rather that note combinations form patterns which are used over and over.

The new rhythm pattern ♩ ♩ ♩ occurs six times, but the notes change direction more frequently, and there is a greater mixture of steps and skips.

PIANO ADVENTURES VIDEO

see it in action

Teaching Video 15

As Patrick discovers, being a "rhythm detective" prepares you for what's ahead. Realizing that the pattern recurs so often makes the piece easy to play.

The adventure begins with a mystery move, a whoosh down to the white keys. Patrick is proud that he remembers to use "rolling fingers".

Another magic move creates Halloween music sung with new words. And at last the Tooth Fairy tiptoes in, high on the keyboard. Isn't transposition fun!

Ask Yourself

■ What does the teacher do while Patrick circles the patterns?

■ Where are Patrick's eyes when he plays?

■ Which new position do you think Patrick likes best? How do you know?

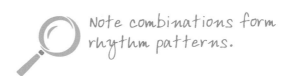

Note combinations form rhythm patterns.

I Hear the Echo

Lesson Book page 20

what's new

- forte and piano

what's important

- Hearing the difference between forte and piano
- Playing forte and piano

let's get started

1 Do you know what an echo is? I'll call out something and you echo me. (Call out the student's name, hello …)

2 In music we say forte, for loud, and piano, for soft. (Shout forte, whisper piano.)

3 Let's sing the melody The More We Get Together to the words Now Let's All Tap It Forte. Tap the beats forte and piano on the cover.

(See Video and Duet Appendix p. 154)

4 Play high Gs with both hands, using braced finger 3s. (Have the student keep the beat while you play When the Saints March Forte In!)

(See Video and Duet Appendix pp. 156-157)

5 Can you find and circle this rhythm pattern in the piece?

6 Let's play. Remember your echo!

explore & create

- **Ear Echoes**
  Place fingers 2-3-4 (both hands) over the 3-black-keys. I'll play a short music message, *forte*. You echo the message, *piano*. Now you create a music message and send it to me.

- **Choose Your Mountain**
  (Move the student's fingers down to F-G-A, C-D-E, or G-A-B.) Let's play echoes on another mountain top.

- **Martian Echoes**
  Put your RH fingers 2-3-4 on the 3-black-keys and your LH fingers 4-3-2 on the white keys (C-D-E). (Play a whole-tone duet.)

(See Video and Duet Appendix p. 158)

 An echo is a good way to describe the difference between forte and piano.

Duet Appendix pp. 154-158   CD Tracks 10-11
8-measure IMPROVISATION at the end.
Students freely play any black keys and explore
f sounds (Mm. 1-4) and *p* sounds (Mm. 5-8).

partner pages

Theory
p. 11 Rhythm A or B? / Echo the Rhythm!

■ Hearing short rhythms as separate and distinct patterns is at the core of this ear-training. The student circles pattern a or b, then circles *f* or *p* for the dynamic mark played.

■ For Ear-Training, play a short, *forte* message on any black key. The student softly echoes. Then reverse with the student as the leader.

Performance
p. 4 Wind in the Trees

■ Holding the damper pedal down throughout gives a special effect for this 2-black-key piece.

■ Coach students to circle the longer rhythm pattern that occurs 3 times.

■ Can students spot the short rhythm pattern beginning line 2?

■ Though legato is not formally taught at the Primer Level, playing LH fingers 2-3 back and forth creates an opportunity to connect the sound.

pedagogy pointers

Dynamics are introduced early so that more sensitive playing is part of the student's musical experience from the outset of study.

The example of an echo is a natural way to teach the difference between forte and piano. Doing this also promotes pattern recognition. The words in the piece reinforce the loud/soft concept, and the echo phrases are true—the notes and rhythms are the same.

 Hearing the difference between forte and piano is ear-training!

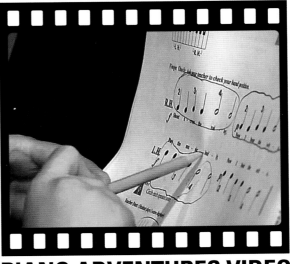

PIANO ADVENTURES VIDEO

see it in action

Teaching Video 16

Both Patrick and David have fun changing dynamics before they are asked to use them while playing a piece. David really enjoys leading those "saints" himself.

The new rhythm pattern is a long one, but it helps Patrick see the shape of the piece and how the pattern is repeated.

Sending music echo messages is another dynamic experience for David that might easily be an ear-training game, too.

Patrick discovers that Martians can create echoes in outer space. A far-out, eerie experience!

Ask Yourself

■ What is the physical difference between tapping forte and tapping piano?

■ What does the teacher do while Patrick is circling the rhythm patterns?

■ Can you think of other ear-training games to reinforce forte and piano?

BASIC RHYTHMS

The Whole Note

Lesson Book page 21

what's new

■ **The Whole Note**

what's important

■ **Feeling whole notes**

■ **Recognizing whole notes**

■ **Understanding the relationship among quarter, half, and whole notes**

let's get started

1 The whole note is a lo-o-o-ng note. (Point to it on the page.) It gets four counts!

2 Let's tap and count whole notes. Now choose any key and let's play and count whole notes.

3 Now we'll sing and play The Whole Note Song. You keep a whole-note beat on high Gs.

(Duet Appendix p. 159)

4 When we draw whole notes, we can sing our song: It's got a head but no stem and it's not colored in.

(Duet Appendix p. 159)

5 Let's tap the Forte and Piano Rhythms drill on the page *forte* and *piano!* Now you play the rhythm on high Cs with my duet.

explore & create

■ **Out for a Slow Walk**
Let's walk across the room using whole notes for each step. Count 1-2-3-4. We can bend our knees as we hold the step.

■ **Walk As You Wish**
What if we wanted to cross the room quickly? Which note would we use: quarter, half, or whole? Suppose we take a lazy walk. Now which note would we use?

■ **The Race Is On!**
(Discuss the story of the tortoise and the hare.) You be the tortoise, and I'll be the hare. We both start at the bottom of the keyboard and aim for the top. But you can only race in whole notes! Do you think you can win?

(See Video)

Making music should come before reading music.

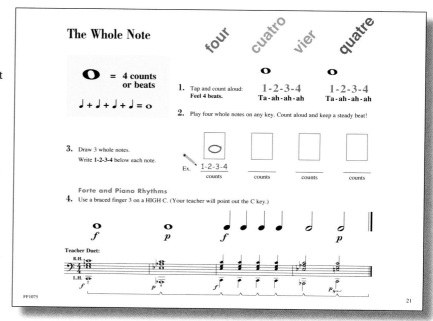

♪🎵 Duet Appendix p. 159

pedagogy pointers

For most young children it's hard to wait a long time. So feeling a whole note may be a challenge.

Once again, it's important to remember that experiencing a whole note—like tapping, clapping, or arm circles—should precede learning what it looks like, or how to draw it.

Note that basic rhythm values are learned before the student is asked to read staff notation, and there is ample reinforcement of rhythm patterns prior to that time, also.

This means that the student has many and varied musical experiences before staff notation is presented.

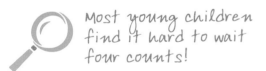

Most young children find it hard to wait four counts!

PIANO ADVENTURES VIDEO

see it in action

Teaching Video 17

Philip first taps, then plays notes that last four counts. The song that's used to draw notes is now familiar, so Philip can anticipate that "it's not colored in". The rhythm drill becomes musical when the fortes and pianos are combined with rich and evocative chords.

Imagine racing in whole notes! The story of the tortoise and the hare comes to life when played on the keyboard. Philip has some doubts that he can win, but that crazy rabbit scoots around sniffing for carrots. The story's true—the tortoise wins!

Ask Yourself

■ When Philip plays loud and soft whole and half notes, he has not yet fully grasped the technical difference involved. What is it?

Old MacDonald Had a Song

Lesson Book pages 22-23

what's new

- ■ **Repeat sign**
- ■ **The melody is divided between the hands**
- ■ **A two-page piece**

what's important

- ■ **Playing a familiar tune**
- ■ **Having fun playing a longer piece**

let's get started

1 There's a piano on this farm! Instead of "moo, moo here", the farmer sings, "black key here".

2 How many times do we use this pattern? (Student may circle.)

♩ ♩ 𝅝

3 How many times do we use this pattern? (Student may circle.)

♩ ♩ ♩ ♩

4 Music uses some shorthand tricks. (Explain the repeat sign.)

5 Let's follow the arrows to see where the melody goes. Be sure to have both hands ready!

explore & create

■ **Your Own Farm Sounds**
Play any black keys you like. Try soft sounds, loud sounds, long sounds, and short sounds. I'll keep the duet going.

(Duet Appendix p. 160, until measure 12)

■ **Improvising Within a Piece**
Let's make a very long piece—like a big sandwich. (A section of original "farm music" is the middle between performances of the whole piece.)

(See Video and Duet Appendix pp. 160-161)

■ **Let's Visit a New Farm**
"Whoosh" both hands down to the white keys. (Play the piece in F.)

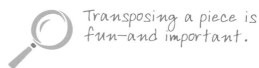

Transposing a piece is fun—and important.

Practice Steps

1. On the **closed keyboard lid,** play and say finger numbers. Feel the whole notes by saying, "**two-oo-oo-oo**" for this finger.
2. On the keyboard, play and count.
3. Play and sing the words.

Find the Keys

3 2   2 3 4
└ L.H. ┘ └ R.H. ┘

Old MacDonald Had a Song

Eye Check: Ask your teacher to watch your eyes as you play. Did you have to look down?

R.H.
𝆑 Old Mac-Don-ald had a song,   e - i - e - i - O (2 - 3 - 4)
Played his key-board all day long,

L.H.

Repeat sign
These dots mean to go back to the beginning and play once again.

22   CD 12-13   12-13   8-9   5

FF1075

BASIC RHYTHMS

Duet Appendix pp. 160-161   CD Tracks 12-13
16-measure IMPROVISATION at the end.
Students explore more free rhythmic
movement on the black keys.

partner pages

Theory
pp. 12-13 The Whole Note

■ Students help the "Farmer, Count Your Bleats" by writing the counts under the rhythms with quarter, half, and whole notes. A Super Student challenge asks students to tap one rhythm while the teacher taps another.

■ Hidden musical terms provide fun investigation and review concepts in Units 1-2.

Technique & Artistry
pp. 8-9 All the Stars Are Shining

■ This piece uses the same hand position as Old MacDonald but presents instead a pedaled, dreamy piece with black-key clusters. Forte and piano echoes can tune up listening skills.

Performance
p. 5 The Shepherd's Flute

■ A pentatonic shepherd melody uses all the note values learned thus far: quarter, half, and whole. Another effective piece for a black-key improvisation with teacher duet.

pedagogy pointers

Old MacDonald is the first piece that divides the melody between the hands. Because the melody shifts frequently from right to left hand, it's important that the hands are both in place at the beginning. There is no need to look down at the fingers. The whole note is reinforced amid quarter and half notes.

The repeat of the opening melody is anticipated, so it's natural to introduce the repeat sign as a shortcut to notate this. This is also the first long piece, but its familiarity and the many repeated patterns make it easy to learn.

PIANO ADVENTURES VIDEO
see it in action

Teaching Video 18

This MacDonald has a piano on his farm, and he plays on the black keys! Discovering the repeated notes and rhythm patterns shows Philip how the piece is put together. Because his fingers are ready over all the keys, he can keep his eyes on the music. Subtle dynamic reminders encourage a musical performance.

Original "farm music" creates a free-for-all middle section of an ABA structure. When his fingers "whoosh" down to the white keys, Philip learns that following patterns makes it easy to play in a new place. E-I-E-I-O!

Ask Yourself

■ When Philip checks out the rhythm patterns, what does he do? Where do you think he learned this?

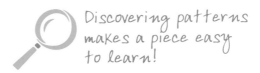 Discovering patterns makes a piece easy to learn!

The Teacher Creates ...

The creative adventure begins with the teacher. An improvised duet is an easy way to model creativity.

Teacher Duets

- Add a spirit of play
- Provide a rhythmic "soundscape"
- Model artistic expression
- Demonstrate hand position and technique

"Fancy Up" the Written Duet

- Add octaves
- Break up the chords
- Take a fragment (one or two measures) and repeat these as a rhythmic "vamp" or use as an introduction
- Change the rhythms
- Change the tempo and/or the mood

By Playing Teacher Duets You

- Convey enthusiasm
- Demonstrate musicality
- Demonstrate technique
- Evoke expressive playing

Get Further Ideas From

- The teaching videos on the DVD
- The Explore & Create section of this text
- The title of the piece
- A story connected to the piece
- A short musical motive from the duet or the piece
- The illustration in the student lesson book

Recognize the power of non-verbal teaching. Students learn by watching and listening.

- Display excellent technique
- Play expressively and rhythmically
- Show enthusiasm and spontaneity

Check out the teacher videos for improvisation samples and ideas.

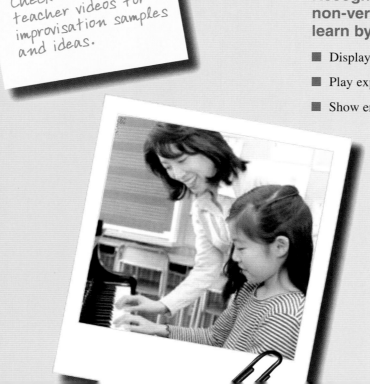

CREATIVITY

The Student Creates ...

Students love to create their own sounds.
The Piano Adventures Teacher encourages students
to express themselves.

The Typical Piano Student

- Plays only what is on the page
- Believes composing is magic, not craft
- Is told not to "play around" at the keyboard
- Feels piano study is serious business

Use "Seeds" (Ideas) from the Piece

- Limitations invite creativity. Freedom overwhelms.
- The "seed" should be short and simple.
- The "seed" could come from the piece.
- The "seed" could come from the title or illustration.

Don't be afraid to let students "loose". The process of exploring sound is more important than what is played.

- Let students use finger and rhythm patterns that they don't yet "know".
- Using rhythmic and melodic patterns creatively helps the student internalize them.

The Piano Adventures Student

- Improvises often
- Plays written music and creates unwritten music
- Is encouraged to create and is supported while doing so
- Has fun at the keyboard

The "Seed" Might Be

- A theoretical concept—an interval, black-key "scale" ...
- A rhythm—a rhythmic value, a new rhythm pattern ...
- An ostinato—using a pattern from the piece ...
- A "takeoff" from the piece—a meow, space message ...

Creative seeds can come from the piece, title, or illustration.

KEY NAMES

The Music Alphabet

Lesson Book page 24

what's new
■ Names for the white keys

what's important
■ Be able to play and say the music alphabet forward and backward

let's get started

1 In music we use only a part of the alphabet: A-B-C-D-E-F-G.

2 We begin at the very bottom of the keyboard. (Use a braced third finger. Play several octaves to demonstrate.)

3 Make an "O" by bracing LH finger 3 with your thumb. Start on the lowest key. Play and say the names of the keys.

4 When you get to the middle, switch to the right hand. Go all the way to the top! Keep saying the notes aloud. Use this alphabet rhythm over and over:

A B C D E F G

explore & create

■ **Alphabet Rap!**
Here's the chant with a fancier rhythm.

A B C D E F G

Let's clap and say it. Start low and play to the top. I'll play a cool duet with you.

(See Video and Duet Appendix p. 162)

■ **Backward Rap!**
Let's cheer! Say and clap after me:

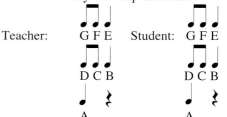
Teacher: G F E   Student: G F E
D C B   D C B
A   A

■ **Backward Rap on the Keys!**
Let's do the Backward Rap, starting at the top, then going down the keyboard. I'll make a different jazzy duet with you.

(Duet Appendix p. 163)

G F E   D C B   A!

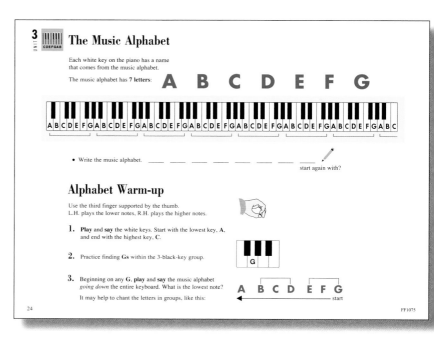

3 UNIT CDEFGAB **The Music Alphabet**

Each white key on the piano has a name that comes from the music alphabet.

The music alphabet has **7 letters**: **A B C D E F G**

ABCDEFGABCDEFGABCDEFGABCDEFGABCDEFGABCDEFGABCDEFGABC

• Write the music alphabet. ___ ___ ___ ___ ___ ___ ___
start again with?

Alphabet Warm-up

Use the third finger supported by the thumb.
L.H. plays the lower notes, R.H. plays the higher notes.

1. **Play** and **say** the white keys. Start with the lowest key, **A**, and end with the highest key, **C**.

2. Practice finding **Gs** within the 3-black-key group.

G

3. Beginning on any **G**, **play** and **say** the music alphabet *going down* the entire keyboard. What is the lowest note?
It may help to chant the letters in groups, like this:

← A B C D E F G — start

24   FF1075

♪♫ Duet Appendix pp. 162-163

pedagogy pointers

Since the music alphabet uses only seven letters, they can all be learned at once. What makes it even easier is that the lowest keyboard note is A. So zooming up the keyboard from bottom to top, saying the letter names, does the trick. It's a good idea to practice them backwards, too.

This is primarily just an orientation to the white-key names, but it gives the student the satisfaction of covering the entire keyboard.

Repeating the seven-letter series also unlocks some of the mystery of keyboard geography. The association of certain key names with black-key groupings will be demonstrated in the pieces to come.

 Finding the music alphabet on the white keys is a "big idea" that is introduced as a "whole".

PIANO ADVENTURES VIDEO

see it in action

Teaching Video 19

Kai uses braced third fingers—another way to reinforce a rounded hand shape. But the fun really begins when she gets to "rap out" the music alphabet as part of a groovy duet.

Saying and playing the alphabet backwards does not come so naturally. Another chant, one that breaks up the alphabet in sections, gets Tatiana ready to play and say the key names in reverse. The jazzy accompaniment keeps everything swinging and hopping—including Tatiana's whole body! Who doesn't like to be a cheerleader?

Ask Yourself

■ What do you notice about how Kai and Tatiana play on the white keys?

■ How can you tell that Tatiana has internalized the rhythm pattern?

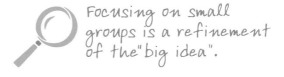 Focusing on small groups is a refinement of the "big idea".

Balloons

Lesson Book page 25

what's new

- ■ C-D-E related to the 2-black-keys
- ■ Piece on the white keys
- ■ Hand crossings

what's important

- ■ Finding C-D-E all over the keyboard
- ■ Smooth and graceful cross-overs
- ■ Steady tempo

let's get started

1 Here's an easy way to find C-D-E. Look for the 2-black-key group. C-D-E are the keys directly underneath. (Help the student find some groups.)

2 Circle all the 2-black-keys. Write C-D-E on the white keys.

3 (On the closed keyboard cover, then on C-D-E.) Let your LH rise slowly, as if it were attached to a balloon. Let it come back down slowly and gently.

(See Video)

4 Let your LH rise and float over the RH. Your RH can then float out from under and move higher, too.

(See Video)

5 Just as these C-D-E groups float up the page, so your balloons will float to the top of the keyboard. (Demonstrate)

6 Let's float gently with a duet!

(Duet Appendix p. 164)

explore & create

■ **Pop Your Balloons!**
When you finish the piece, let your RH push off the C-D-E cluster, popping your balloon.

■ **Happy Landing!**
Start at the top and let the balloons float happily to the ground—E-D-C, E-D-C, etc. Play a jaunty duet.

(Duet Appendix p. 165)

■ **Hide and Seek**
Put your RH fingers 2-3-4 over C-D-E and close your eyes. I'll play some short patterns. You can copy me!

(Try some using the LH.)

■ **Trick the Teacher**
Play some patterns using C-D-E for me and see if I can copy you!

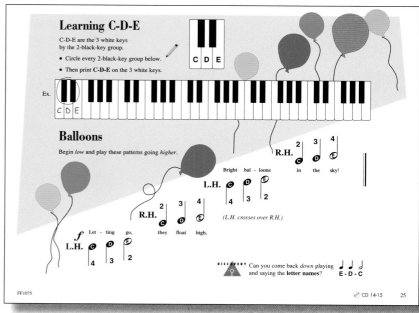

 Duet Appendix pp. 164-165   CD Tracks 14-15
4-measure IMPROVISATION at the end.
Students freely play any high white keys.

pedagogy pointers

This first piece for the white keys teaches C-D-E as a group. It also directs the student's eyes to move up the page just as the hands move up the keyboard. Playing with the middle fingers directs the weight toward the center of the hand.

Since this is the first time the hands cross over each other to go higher, the gestures involved should be prepared. This can be done on the closed keyboard cover before trying the gestures on the keys. The hand must first rise and sink gently, as if tied to a balloon.

This preparation eliminates the need to look for specific C-D-E groups—a good way to begin.

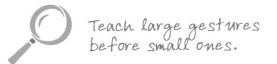

Teach large gestures before small ones.

PIANO ADVENTURES VIDEO

see it in action

Teaching Video 20

Hannah and Emily test their balloons in place first, but soon see how the balloons cross over and float out from under. Once the moves are prepared, it's time to try the piece. Don't forget to float back to your lap! Since the teacher holds down the pedal, those balloons really shimmer.

Hannah brings the balloons down, and the peppy duet helps them sink quickly.

Emily listens intently and copies those patterns without missing a trick. Her eyes are shut, but her ears are wide open!

Ask Yourself

■ Which do you think is more effective—what the teacher says, or what the teacher does?

■ How does the teacher sequence the ear-training? Is there much talking?

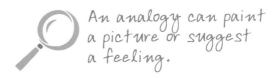

An analogy can paint a picture or suggest a feeling.

Merrily We Roll Along

Lesson Book page 26

what's new

- ■ **This C-D-E melody for RH and LH uses steps and repeated notes**

what's important

- ■ **Using a rounded hand shape on the white keys**
- ■ **Tracking notes on the page without looking at the hands**

let's get started

1 Circle each time this rhythm pattern is used in this piece:

2 Find C-D-E groups with fingers 2-3-4. Let's play a game! You put your hands in your lap. I'll count with closed eyes. How fast can you find the position and shout, "Ready!"

3 Play and keep hands rounded like the sun in the picture. Pretend a little boat is under each hand!

4 Play with the duet. (Play an "intro" of the last two measures to set the tempo. Together, gently lift hands into lap at the end.) Now try it again while I play a trickier accompaniment. (Duet Appendix p. 166)

explore & create

- ■ **Sail on 3-Black Keys**
  "Sail" fingers 2-3-4 onto the 3-black keys. Play again.

- ■ **Sail to F-G-A**
  Let the wind blow the sailboat down the lake. Help students "swoosh" fingers to F-G-A and play again.

- ■ **Sail to G-A-B**
  The wind kicks up! "Swoosh" fingers 2-3-4 higher to G-A-B and play again.

- ■ **Sail to A-B-C**
  A storm is brewing! "Swoosh" fingers 2-3-4 up to A-B-C. Sing "Scar-i-ly we roll a-long, o'er the deep, dark sea."

(Duet Appendix p. 167)

At this stage pieces can be played in any range.

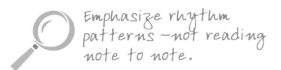
Emphasize rhythm patterns —not reading note to note.

 Duet Appendix pp. 166-167  CD Tracks 16-17

partner pages

Technique & Artistry
pp. 10-11 Merrily I Move Down
Merrily I Move Up

- Discuss memorizing a short musical pattern and how this can be repeated in higher or lower octaves.

- Student memorizes the LH pattern on p. 10 and repeats it lower, keeping a round hand shape.

- Play the RH as a special ending to Merrily We Roll Along, Lesson Book, p. 26. Play a high C as the final note.

Performance
pp. 6-7 Hot Cross Buns

On the closed keyboard lid

- Pretend to sprinkle "yeast" on the student's hands. Let hands rise to form round "hot cross buns".

- Tap the rhythm with rounded hands: Count "1 - 2, 1 - 2, 1 - 2 - 3 - 4," etc. Play hot *forte* and cool *piano* sounds.

- Play the duet with the student at a "quick-bake" tempo. Try for 30 seconds or less!

pedagogy pointers

Awareness of rhythm patterns promotes good reading habits and musicianship. In this piece the use of quarter, half, and whole notes is reinforced, as is movement by steps and repetition. The middle fingers of each hand continue to keep the weight centered.

Awareness of melodic patterns—step up, step down, repeat—also promotes good reading habits and musicianship. This is the basis of fluent playing.

PIANO ADVENTURES VIDEO

see it in action

Teaching Video 21

One of the simplest rhythm patterns is featured in this piece, and David discovers how often it's used. Repeating his performance against different accompaniment styles ensures that his feel for this pattern is secure.

Since the melody uses only the three middle fingers in each hand, David quickly understands that he can play the piece anywhere on the keyboard!

Ask Yourself

- What does the teacher do while David circles the rhythm patterns?

- Where are David's eyes while he plays?

Transposing provides repetition and introduces new sounds—such as playing in a minor key.

The Escalator

Lesson Book page 27

what's new

- ■ F-G-A-B as related to the 3-black-key group

what's important

- ■ Be able to find and play groups of F-G-A-B

- ■ Use fingers 2 and 3 in each hand, keeping a rounded hand shape

- ■ Prepare the hand crossings with good "rainbows"

let's get started

1 The note names right around the 3-black-keys are F-G-A-B.

2 Four friends are going up this escalator: fingers 2 and 3 in each hand.

3 Watch while I give these four friends a smooth ride. (Play the piece and sing the words.)

4 Let's try it. Each hand has to start moving as soon as it's finished playing in order to keep the ride smooth. (You may want to use your own hand to guide the student's eyes and hand to the next group of 3-black-keys.)

5 Did your four friends have a smooth ride on the keyboard escalator?

explore & create

- ■ **Glide Right Up!**
  (Hold the pedal down while the student plays.) Listen to the smooth ride up.

- ■ **Finished Shopping**
  Coming down! Play B-A-G-F down the keyboard.

- ■ **Meeting Friends Halfway**
  You begin at the bottom, and I'll begin at the top. I'll go around you when we meet. (Reverse)

  (See Video)

- ■ **Having a Good Time!**
  When the friends get to the top floor, they have a little giggle. (Trill with fingers 2 and 3.) And they giggle all the way down!

  (See Video)

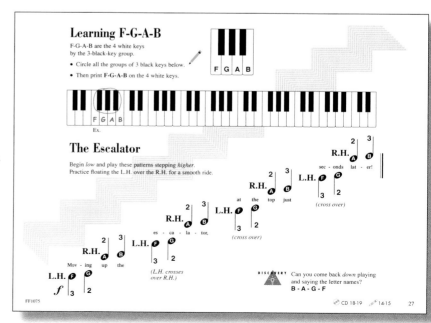

Learning F-G-A-B

F-G-A-B are the 4 white keys by the 3-black-key group.

- Circle all the groups of 3 black keys below.
- Then print **F-G-A-B** on the 4 white keys.

The Escalator

Begin *low* and play these patterns stepping *higher.*
Practice floating the L.H. over the R.H. for a smooth ride.

Mov - ing up the es - ca - la - tor, at the top just sec - onds lat - er!

(L.H. crosses over R.H.) (cross over) (cross over)

DISCOVERY Can you come back *down* playing and saying the letter names? **B - A - G - F**

FF1075   CD 18-19   14-15   27

partner pages

Theory
p. 14 A-MAZE-ING Keys—A B C D E F G

■ Students complete a musical maze to find a "home" for the seven letters of the musical alphabet.

p. 15 Let's Make Alphabet Soup!

■ Make "alphabet soup" by filling in the missing letter names for the music alphabets. Each music alphabet begins on a different letter name—A B C D E F or G. Students drill stepwise reading by chanting the various alphabets going forward and backward.

pedagogy pointers

This piece introduces the student to the white keys associated with the 3-black-key groups.

It's easier to divide the F-G-A-B group between the hands, and using fingers 2 and 3 keeps the hands in balance. Hand crossings are also reinforced.

Care has been taken to ensure that the student does not associate the thumb (RH) or fifth finger (LH) with C, F, or G—as in C Position, F Position, or G Position.

The student begins to understand that any key can be played with any finger.

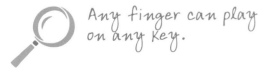

Any finger can play on any key.

PIANO ADVENTURES VIDEO

see it in action

Teaching Video 22

In order to give his four "friends" a smooth ride, Philip needs to look ahead for the new group, releasing and moving each hand as soon as it's finished playing—a fancy and graceful crossover. And when the pedal is down, the escalator glides right up. No wonder those friends have a good giggle all the way down!

As Philip continues to ride the escalator, his fingers loosen up and his hand position improves. Sometimes you meet your friends right in the middle of the ride—you're going up, they're going down—but there's no stopping the escalator. You can only laugh together when you're finished with the trip.

Ask Yourself

■ How does the teacher guide Philip's first attempt to play the piece?

■ The trills played on the way down require a different technique than hand crossings. What is required here?

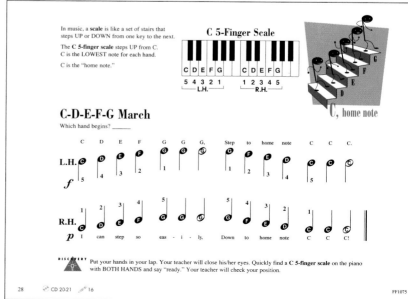

KEY NAMES

C-D-E-F-G March

Lesson Book page 28

what's new

- Steps on the keyboard
- C five-finger scale (C position)
- Playing steps with five fingers

what's important

- Recognizing adjacent keys as steps
- Using adjacent fingers to play steps
- Understanding the C five-finger scale as a concept

let's get started

1 Look at these notes marching up the steps. Point to them while I step up the keyboard.

2 The notes step up, like the steps of a ladder. We call that a scale. The word "scale" comes from the word for "ladder".

3 Place your RH thumb on C. Then step up the C five-finger scale. Place your LH fifth finger on C. Then step up the C five-finger scale.

4 Look at the piece. Point to some repeated notes. Which notes are stepping? Point to the notes while I play the entire piece.

5 Now I'll point while you play. Which hand begins?

explore & create

- **Stretch Out!**
  Play the LH one octave lower, or the RH one octave higher—or both!

- **Rock 'n Roll March**
  Can you keep a steady tempo while I play some rock sounds?

  (Duet Appendix p. 168)

- **Outer Space March**
  This march is slower. Listen to the mysterious outer space music. I'll play a "Martian" accompaniment.

  (Duet Appendix p. 168)

- **Ear Tunes**
  Put your RH fingers over the C five-finger scale. Close your eyes. I'll play a short pattern (one octave lower). See if you can copy me.

- **Ear Tunes for the Left Hand**
  Repeat the Ear Tunes Game. (The Ear Tunes Games could also be played in lessons following the presentation of this piece.)

♪♫ Duet Appendix p. 168    CD Tracks 20-21
8-measure IMPROVISATION at the end. Students
freely play notes from the C five-finger scale.

partner pages

Theory
p. 16 C Scale Ladders

■ Students complete C Scale Ladders to spell
the C five-finger scale, then help Quarter
Note Guy "step to the beach" by writing the
correct letter names on the sandy "C scale
path". Playing the tune with each hand completes the activity.

pedagogy pointers

Here's the first chance to use all five fingers,
in each hand, playing on the white keys. The
unstaffed notation is a clear picture of a rise
and descent with repeated notes at the top and
bottom.

The C five-finger scale is a new concept, and
it's prepared well in advance of reading five-
finger patterns on the staff. This is the natural
order of learning—the experience comes before
the definition.

 A scale is a ladder. We can step up and down the ladder with our fingers.

PIANO ADVENTURES VIDEO

see it in action

Teaching Video 23

A scale, like a ladder, is meant for climbing, and the
notes step up from C to G. Vivian's steps are steady
and the dynamic changes are carefully noted. When
the march starts rockin' 'n rollin', she enjoys the fun
and the challenge of holding her own. The marching
"Martians" make a wonderful contrast and accustom
the young player to less predictable sounds. Why not
visit outer space?

Ask Yourself

■ What does the teacher do when she demonstrates
the piece?

■ What helps the student prepare for playing the
piece?

Men From Mars

Lesson Book page 29

what's new

- Measures
- Bar lines

what's important

- Understanding how rhythms are organized
- Playing repeated notes and steps is reinforced

let's get started

1 Perhaps your kitchen dishes are organized in certain piles, or the shoes are lined up in your closet. In music we organize notes into measures.

2 (Lead the student through the text at the top of the page, teaching measure and bar line.)

3 Let's add up the beats in each measure of the piece.

4 Now let's circle all the repeated notes for the Martians.

5 Where do the notes step down? Step up?

6 Put both hands over the C five-finger scale. You're ready to go!

Kids love outer space sounds!

explore & create

- **Can You Add Up to Four?**
  Here we'll write note combinations that add to four. (Help the student count them.)

- **Can You Write Up to Four?**
  Let's see how many different rhythms we can write that will add up to four.

- **Martian Conversation**
  Suppose "three green men" had a conversation in outer space. I'll play three notes anywhere on the keyboard. Your "three green men" can answer anywhere, too. (Keep the pedal down for an "outer space" sound.)

  (See Video)

- **Would You Like to Go to Mars?**
  Would you like to go to Mars? Check out mars.jpl.nasa.gov/kids. Pack your spaceship and then blast off. How about some moon cookies?

CD Tracks 22-23
8-measure IMPROVISATION at the end.
Students explore "Martian sounds" (any
black or white keys) on the keyboard.

partner pages

Theory
p. 17 Who's Your Favorite Martian?

■ Students divide the music into measures, draw
bar lines and play the C five-finger scale song. A
Martian Musician asks to hear the student's own
Martian tune!

Technique & Artistry
pp. 12-13 Basketball Dribble

■ Stand and pretend to bounce a basketball.
Notice the large up and down motion of
your wrist.

■ Now pretend to bounce the basketball quickly.
What happens to the motion of the wrist? (Coach
the student to realize that it becomes smaller.)

■ Play Basketball Dribble bracing finger 3 with
the thumb. Bounce your ball up and down the
keyboard.

Performance
p. 8 Banana Split

■ Circle the repeated notes.

■ Which two measures are like Basketball
Dribble?

■ Rhythm Ideas: Student taps the rhythm while
you play the duet. Student taps LH while you
tap RH. Then reverse.

■ Student plays. Keep hand round like a scoop
of ice cream.

pedagogy pointers

Playing a C five-finger scale is combined with
repeating many of the notes. The way the notes
step up or down is also more subtle than in previous pieces. Thus, reinforcement of several learned
concepts is fused in a new context.

Measures and bar lines are introduced. Since the
student has been playing many pieces combining
quarter and half notes in repeated rhythm patterns,
it is not difficult to explain how rhythms and
rhythm patterns are organized. Once again,
experiencing a concept precedes defining it.

PIANO ADVENTURES VIDEO

see it in action

Teaching Video 24

These aliens walk carefully, often repeating before
they continue up or down. Checking to see where
the notes repeat prepares Patrick to play the piece.
Imagining tiny Martians under his palms reminds
him to play with a rounded hand position. Because
his hands are in place before he begins, he can keep
his eyes on the music.

Finding outer space notes for "three green men"
creates a musical Martian language. Patrick's "men"
really shoot high and low. Maybe they're on their
way to the moon!

Ask Yourself

■ When is the only time that Patrick looks down at
his hands?

■ Could you think of other ways to create outer
space music?

 First the experience—
then the definition.

59

Ode to Joy

Lesson Book page 30

what's new

- New dynamic mark—*mf*
- Music by an important classical composer

what's important

- Playing *mf*
- Recognizing the differences among *f*, *p*, and *mf*

let's get started

1 (Play measures 1-4 of the piece *p*, then *f*, each time asking the student to identify the dynamic level.) What if we wanted to play somewhere in between? (Introduce *mezzo forte*.)

2 Circle all the repeated notes.

3 Let's compare the RH and LH melodies. Which measure is different?

4 Almost every note is a quarter note. Where does that change?

5 Play the first line of the piece *p*, then *f*, then *mf*.

explore & create

- **I'm Home**
  A melody that uses the C five-finger scale can begin on any note, but it usually ends on the "home note", C.

- **Where's Home?**
  Let's check this. Does Ode to Joy end on C? Check C-D-E-F-G March (p. 28). How does it end? Check Men from Mars (p. 29). How does it end?

- **Ears Open**
  (Play short musical examples for student to identify *f*, *mf*, or *p*.)

- **Time Travel**
  Would you like to find out what was Beethoven's favorite food? It might be your favorite food, too. Check out dsokids.com, click on the boombox, and then click on Beethoven's name.

partner pages

Technique & Artistry
p. 14 Going to the North Pole

■ We are going to let our fingers play in the snow and travel up the keys to the North Pole.

■ First, we'll sink deep into the snow (demonstrate ♩ notes). Then tromp steadily (demonstrate ♩ notes). When we play the snowball whole note, watch your thumb, then shift it quickly to the next key. Are you doing a "thumb perch"?

■ Play an octave lower with the student to model a round hand shape. On the whole note, check for "round snowball hands" before starting the next pattern.

Performance
p. 9 Train's A-Comin'

■ Ask the student to look carefully at the music and find a C five-finger scale going up, then going down.

■ Play with the duet. Pretend the train is coming into the station and slow down for the last three measures.

pedagogy pointers

Music gains interest with a variety of dynamics. Forte and piano provide a good contrast, and it's easy for a young player to exaggerate these differences. But much music is played in between these levels—*mezzo forte*.

At the piano, dynamics are created by using more or less energy and speed when pressing down the keys, so it's a technical challenge for the student to play medium loud.

Playing mezzo forte is also a matter of ear-training. It takes more careful listening to judge when sounds are between loud and soft. Play at different dynamic levels for students and ask them to report what they hear.

PIANO ADVENTURES VIDEO

see it in action

Teaching Video 25

With this piece, Patrick begins to refine his sense of dynamics by hearing and feeling what it means to play medium-loud sounds. This famous melody requires rich, but not forceful, tone. By first playing soft, then loud, Patrick learns to gauge how much energy to use when playing *mf*. He proves his new skill by changing dynamics on call, by hearing differences, and by creating his own sounds.

Ask Yourself

■ How would you describe the differences among Patrick's attempts to play piano, then forte, then mezzo forte?

■ How does Patrick's performance improve as he continues to play the piece?

■ What's particularly interesting when Patrick is asked to describe which dynamics he hears?

 Make sure the student hears the difference between loud and soft.

Sea Story

Lesson Book page 31

what's new

- A melody that includes C-B-A-G-F in the left hand
- The left hand is over a different five-finger scale than the right

what's important

- Reading and playing the down and up direction of the notes

let's get started

1 Point to the notes while I play. Watch out! It's pretty wavy on this boat.

2 Where are the notes stepping down? Stepping up? Where do they repeat? Where do the notes step up and down?

3 Put your LH thumb on a lower C and play five notes down. Your left hand is now over a different five-finger scale.

4 Let's try the piece. Which hand begins? This time I'll point to the notes while you play.

explore & create

- **Drifting Apart**
  Try playing the right hand one octave higher. Keep your left hand in the low octave.

- **Slow Rowboat**
  Let's take a slow row so that we can see all the scenery. I'll come along with the duet.

- **Motor Boat**
  Let's put a motor on this boat and take a zippy ride together across the lake.

- **Motor Trouble!**
  Listen as we play. My motor might develop trouble and slow down. See if you can follow me. Or I might rev the engine and speed up. Can you hang in there and follow my boat?

  (See Video)

- **You're the Captain**
  You can manage the motor boat. Let's see if I can follow you.

  (See Video)

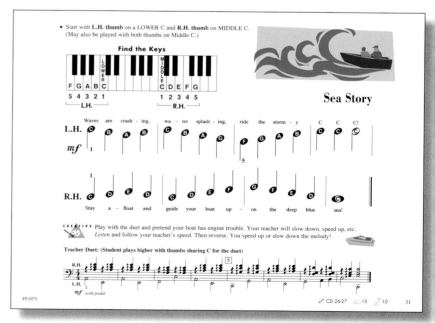

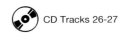

partner pages

Technique & Artistry
p. 15 Going to the South Pole

- Now, with LH, let's take a snow journey on white keys down to the South Pole.
- Sink deep in the snow for the notes, then tromp steadily for the notes.
- For the snowball note, watch your thumb, then shift quickly to the next key.
- Play an octave higher with the student to model a round hand shape. On each note, check for round snowball hands before starting the next pattern.

Performance
p. 10 A Song About Cats

- Circle all the repeated notes.
- Find three measures that are just like measures 1-3.
- Play. Can you keep your eyes on the notes and never look at your hands?

pedagogy pointers

This is the first piece in which the left hand steps down from C to F. Thus the left hand is over a different five-finger scale than the right. Once more care is taken to ensure that the student doesn't get "locked into hand positions".

Playing the hands one octave apart helps the student maintain a more natural and relaxed position at the keyboard.

PIANO ADVENTURES VIDEO

see it in action

Teaching Video 26

We're off on an exciting boat ride. The notes change direction more frequently, making waves on the page and in the hand, so it's good to check out the movements before playing. We don't want the boat crashing in the waves!

But then the motor on the boat starts to stall, and the ride slows down until we rev up the engine again. Both Vivian and Tatiana have fun with flexing the tempo, either as a passenger in the boat, or as the driver. This kind of ear-training requires very sensitive listening. Bon voyage!

Ask Yourself

- When Vivian first tries the piece, there are certain hesitations and errors. Why do these occur where they do?
- When Vivian and Tatiana control the speed, each has the most fun doing what?

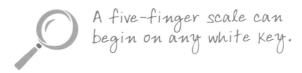 A five-finger scale can begin on any white key.

KEY NAMES

Hey, Mr. Half Note Dot!

Lesson Book page 32

what's new

- **The Dotted Half Note**

what's important

- **Feeling dotted half notes**
- **Recognizing dotted half notes**
- **Understanding the relationship among dotted half notes, half notes, and quarter notes**

explore & create

- **The Left Hand Is a Very Big Dancer**
  Play the left hand one octave lower, forte. Feel your fingertips.

- **The Right Hand Is a Dancing Elf**
  Play the right hand one octave higher, piano.

- **Dance With a Friend**
  (Have another student play Gs, one octave apart, higher on the keyboard. Play left-right-right, loud-soft-soft.)

let's get started

1 This is a half note, but it has a dot next to it. If we say half-note-dot, how many beats is that?

2 Let's draw some dotted half notes. Here's the chant: It's got a head and a stem and a dot at the end.

(Duet Appendix p. 169)

3 Brace finger 3s and find two high Gs. Play steady dotted half notes and I'll join with Chopsticks.

(See Video and Duet Appendix pp. 170-171)

4 Point to all the dotted half notes. (Point to the half note.) How many counts for this note?

5 Set your left-hand thumb on C below Middle C and your right-hand thumb on Middle C. I'll point to the notes while you play. Ready for the piece!

64

 Duet Appendix pp. 169-171

 CD Tracks 28-29
8-measure IMPROVISATION at the end.
Student plays any white keys with the
3/4 accompaniment.

partner pages

Theory
p. 18 The Dotted Half Note

■ Students draw and write the counts for
quarter, half, dotted half, and whole notes.
Tapping a steady beat and counting aloud
completes the activity.

pedagogy pointers

Most music in 3/4 meter has a dance-like quality
unless the tempo is very slow. Introducing the
dotted half note, then, is easy if it is heard and
played in a lilting musical context—one to the
bar.

Once again, feeling the dotted half note is the
key factor. To make sure the note values learned
so far are distinguished from one another, the
piece includes a half note at a natural place in
the final cadence.

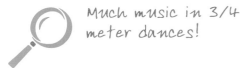 Much music in 3/4
meter dances!

PIANO ADVENTURES VIDEO

see it in action

Teaching Video 27

David enjoys playing those Gs as part of the
Chopsticks team. As David's left hand plays in lower
octaves, it's easy to play up the contrast between a
forte bass dancer and a softer, more graceful right-
hand partner.

And what boy doesn't like to stretch things to the
limit? Extreme fun!

Ask Yourself

■ How would you describe David's hand position
when he plays the repeated Gs?

■ In the Chopsticks duet, what's noticeable about
the teacher's accompaniment?

Alouette

Lesson Book page 33

what's new

- ■ **Playing the dotted half note as part of a familiar song**

what's important

- ■ **Holding the dotted half note for the full three counts**
- ■ **Being ready for the quick changes of direction in Mm. 3-4 and Mm. 7-8**

let's get started

1 How many counts does the dotted half note get? The Alouette bird sits for three counts before she takes off.

2 Listen to the pattern of her name. (Play and sing.) But before we can catch her, she flies up an octave. I'll play and sing her name, moving up to higher Cs each time.

(See Video)

3 Let's see you play her name. I'll try to catch your Alouette bird as you fly your hand to higher Cs.

4 The other part of Alouette's song has quick steps and skips. (Practice the RH in Mm. 3-4 and Mm. 7-8.)

5 What's the only note the left hand plays? Let's fit it into the music.

explore & create

- ■ **Quick Alouette Bird**
  (Encourage the quick feel of this rhythm.)

- ■ **Alouette Flies High**
  Play the piece in the highest octave.
  (Accompany like a music box.)

- ■ **Alouette Flies Away!**
  (Show the student how to play a short glissando from the second highest C to the top.) After playing the piece in the highest octave, Alouette does a glissando.

- ■ **Je Te Plumerai, la Tête**
  After you play the piece, I'll play the middle part of the tune. Then join me again to end the song.

Anticipate a tricky part. Rehearse it ahead of time so it's ready to go!

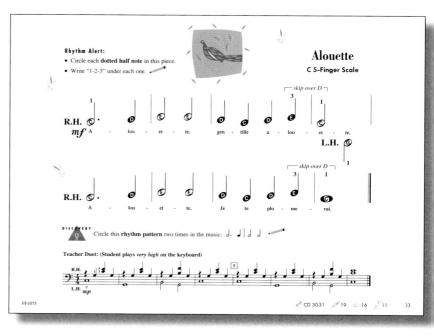

partner pages

Theory
p. 19 What's the Dynamic Mark?

■ Play short musical examples for the student. Listening for dynamics—*p*, *mf*, or *f*—is the focus of this activity.

Technique & Artistry
p. 16 A Special Ending for Alouette

■ Pretend Alouette is flying to the top of the tree. Coach to lift gently with the wrist as the bird flies up and gently lands on the next higher D.

■ As Alouette flies higher and farther away, the music becomes softer!

■ Lean (don't scoot) to reach the highest notes. Slow down and watch for firm fingertips!

Performance
p. 11 School Bell Is Ringing!

■ Guide students to see the sequential pattern, "5 step down, 4 step down, 3 step down," etc.

■ Can LH finger 3 be round as a bell when it rings the dotted half notes?

pedagogy pointers

In Alouette, the new dotted half note is used in a 4/4 meter. It's helpful to tap, clap, or drum the rhythm and count 1-2-3-1, 1-2, 1-2 before playing it with the notes. Pretending that the bird flies to higher octaves is an easy way to repeat the rhythm pattern that includes the dotted half note.

Measures 3-4 and measures 7-8 change direction quickly and require some finger independence and coordination. Prepare these in advance so that, when played in the piece, the first performance is correct. You can help the student avoid stumbles and struggles. This also shows them how to practice!

PIANO ADVENTURES VIDEO

see it in action

Teaching Video 28

Alouette hops gently in a little twisting pattern. Since the melody in measures 3 and 4 is a bit tricky, Olivia takes extra time to prepare it. It's tempting to peek, so covering her hands shows her she can play without looking down. The duet proves that she trusts her fingers to play on their own.

This little bird can fly with its eyes closed—rhythm drill and ear-training combined! Hannah picks up the tempo and demonstrates her skill in using different dynamics. And—surprise—Alouette flutters her wings and flies off on her own!

Ask Yourself

■ Why do you think Olivia sometimes looks down at her fingers when she plays the piece?

■ How does the teacher sequence the ear-training with Olivia?

Notions about Motions

**Some technical principles are basic.
Establish good habits — right from the start.**

Technique Secret: Arm Weight

- Basis for good tone production at the piano
- Takes the burden off the fingers
- Uses gravity to overcome the weight of the key

Heavy Wet Ropes

- Let the arms hang from the shoulders
- Arms remain heavy while the arms are lifted
- Arms drop into the lap

Technique Secret: Braced Finger 3

- Useful to support a weak fingertip
- Rounds the hand and the arch
- Invites a drop of arm weight

Any finger can play any note!

Making O's

- Bring any fingertip to the thumb. Look for the "O"
- Ideal hand position for dropping arm weight into the key
- Helps to align the arm, hand, and finger

Integration

- Tall knuckles over the playing finger provide a platform for balancing the arm
- Arm, hand, and playing finger need to be in a straight line (in alignment)
- Then arm weight can flow into the fingertip
- Bracing a finger with the thumb can help find optimal alignment

Lay a foundation to help the student develop a natural, problem-free technique. Get it right from the start!

TECHNIQUE

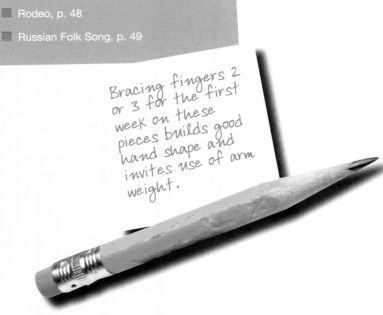

Varied Fingerings

As new notes are introduced, fingerings vary to promote note reading and proper technique.

- Middle C March uses fingers 1, 2, and 3 for Middle C.

- Treble G and Bass Clef F are played with finger 3 as often as with finger 5 (Best Friends, My Invention, and others).

- Frogs on Logs uses a sequential fingerng to promote note reading over hand-position dependence.

For note reading

- Varied fingering prevents the student from equating notes with finger numbers.

- The student is presented with a limited set of notes to learn, but without a fixed, preset hand position.

For technique

- Varied fingering prevents a rigid, fixed hand placement.

- The frequent use of finger 3, as in My Invention, The Dance Band, Rodeo, and Let's Play Ball!, invites a drop of arm weight into a balanced hand.

Remember—

- These are sophisticated concepts that will be revisited in different ways at higher levels

- At this stage the student need not be concerned with technical details

- Don't expect perfect execution every time

- The Pecking Hen/Rooster, pp. 8-9
- Best Friends, p. 39
- My Invention, p. 41
- The Dance Band, p. 44
- Frogs on Logs, p. 45
- Let's Play Ball!, p. 46
- Rodeo, p. 48
- Russian Folk Song, p. 49

Bracing fingers 2 or 3 for the first week on these pieces builds good hand shape and invites use of arm weight.

The Grand Staff

Lesson Book page 34

what's new

- Staff
- Line and space notes
- Grand Staff

what's important

- Recognition of line and space numbering
- Equating the high staff with the RH, the low staff with the LH

let's get started

1 (Use a large Grand Staff without clefs. Show the student how to number the lines and spaces.)

2 For the top staff, I'll call for a line. You point to it. (Do the same for spaces.)

3 For the bottom staff, I'll call for a line. You point to it. (Do the same for spaces.)

4 Let's mix them up. (Call first for the top or bottom staff, then the number of the line or space.)

5 (Explain line notes and space notes. Use the example in the book, notes on the large Grand Staff, or other music in the book.) Is this a line or a space note? How about this one? (Continue)

6 Put your RH on the top staff, your LH on the bottom staff. The RH plays notes on the top staff, the LH plays notes on the bottom staff.

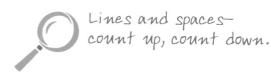

Lines and spaces—count up, count down.

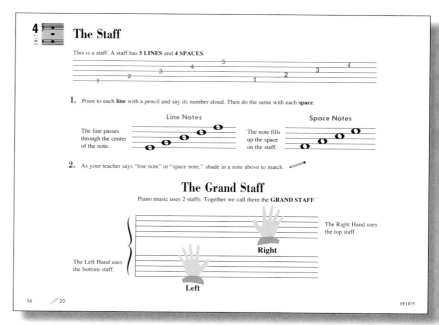

The Staff

This is a staff. A staff has **5 LINES** and **4 SPACES**.

1. Point to each **line** with a pencil and say its number aloud. Then do the same with each **space**.

Line Notes

The line passes through the center of the note.

Space Notes

The note fills up the space on the staff.

2. As your teacher says "line note" or "space note," shade in a note above to match.

The Grand Staff

Piano music uses 2 staffs. Together we call them the **GRAND STAFF**.

The Right Hand uses the top staff.

Right

The Left Hand uses the bottom staff.

Left

34   20

FF1075

Duet Appendix p. 172

explore & create

■ **Sing Your Lines and Spaces**
Point with your finger to the third line. Point with your finger to the fourth space. (Continue)

(Duet Appendix p. 172)

■ **Let's Change Places**
I'll point and you tell me which line or space it is.

■ **Put It There!**
(Have the student draw whole notes on the staff.) Draw a whole note on the top staff, line two. Now draw a whole note on the bottom staff, line three. (Continue)

■ **Hands Up!**
(See Video for an example of how to play this game.)

partner pages

Theory
p. 20 The Staff

■ Students review the staff as they number the lines and spaces, identify line and space notes, and form Grand Staves with bar lines and braces.

pedagogy pointers

The transference of reading from unstaffed notation to reading notes on the staff is carefully planned. By this time the student can read and play quarter, half, dotted half, and whole notes and notes that move by step.

The student also knows the names of the white keys. Now it's time to connect these elements to the staff. The Grand Staff is introduced without clefs.

PIANO ADVENTURES VIDEO

see it in action

Teaching Video 29

Lines and spaces are numbered and Olivia is ready to find specific lines or spaces on her own. Now it's time to learn the difference between line and space notes, and this goes smoothly, too.

The Grand Staff (at the beginning, at least) tells you which hand to use, even without clefs. Philip and Patrick have fun getting their hands in place, and especially putting it all together for the Grand Staff. Hands up!

Ask Yourself

■ Why do you think the teacher has chosen Mister Bluebird to point out the difference between line and space notes?

■ Why do Patrick and Philip enjoy the Grand Staff game? Why is this an effective way to teach the Grand Staff?

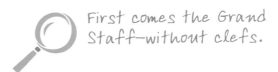

First comes the Grand Staff—without clefs.

Bass Clef and Treble Clef

Lesson Book page 35

what's new

- **Bass clef**
- **Treble clef**

what's important

- **The bass clef shows all the notes below Middle C**
- **The treble clef shows all the notes above Middle C**
- **Tracking notes on the page without looking at the hands**

let's get started

1 A key unlocks a door. Or there can be a key to solving a puzzle. The key that unlocks the mystery of how to read music is called a clef, a sign that helps you find the names of the notes.

2 Have you heard of a bass drum, or a string bass? These instruments make low sounds.

3 On the piano, low sounds are written in the bass clef. (Show the clef.)

4 Think of the sounds made by a flute, or a violin. These instruments make high sounds.

5 On the piano, high sounds are written in the treble clef. (Show the clef.)

6 Together the bass clef and treble clef help you find the names of the notes on the Grand Staff.

A general introduction provides a frame. Details come later.

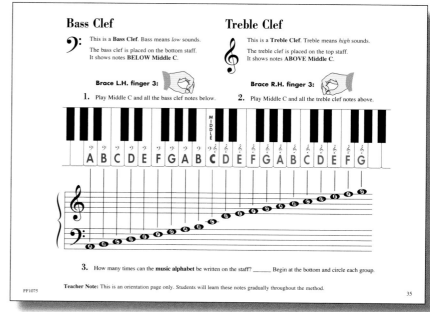

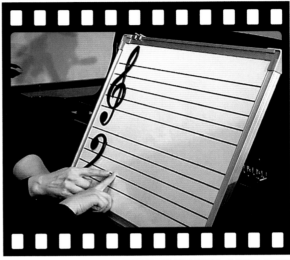
Duet Appendix p. 173

explore & create

■ **Sing Your Lines and Spaces**

Now I'll add the clefs to this game. On the treble clef—Point with your finger to the fifth line. On the bass clef—Point with your finger to the first space. (Continue)

(See Video and Duet Appendix p. 173)

■ **Let's Change Places**

I'll point and you tell me the clef and which line or space it is.

■ **Ear Detective**

(Give the student a big bass clef and treble clef.) Turn around (away from the piano). I'll play some sounds. If they're high sounds, hold up the treble clef. If they're low sounds, hold up the bass clef. (Later, you might play some high and low sounds together to see if the student will hold up both clefs!)

pedagogy pointers

The student has learned what a staff is, and has also begun to associate the top staff with the right hand and the bottom staff with the left. When the bass and treble clefs are introduced, it's important to associate them with low and high sounds, as well as with hands or note names.

Here, the placement of note names on the staff is only a general orientation, used to show how the seven-letter music alphabet fits across the Grand Staff from bottom to top. Connection of note names with Middle C or with specific clefs follows in the pages to come.

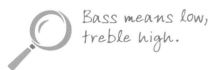

Bass means low, treble high.

PIANO ADVENTURES VIDEO

see it in action

Teaching Video 30

Bass and treble clefs are related to low and high sounds, not just introduced as symbols to distinguish the upper from the lower staff. Santa Claus and the Tooth Fairy are good representatives of each clef, and David has no trouble identifying other high and low "voices" or music examples played in different ranges.

When the music alphabet (see pp. 48-49 and the teaching video) was introduced, the student played these note names across the entire keyboard. David now begins to associate the note names with the bass and treble clefs. Seeing that three complete music alphabets march up and across the Grand Staff gives David a general idea of where these notes are written, as well as where they are found on the keyboard.

Ask Yourself

■ Can you think of other "voices" to associate with bass and treble sounds?

■ When David plays the music alphabet across the keyboard, how does he do so?

Middle C March

Lesson Book page 36

what's new

- ■ **Reading from the Grand Staff**
- ■ **Changing fingers on Middle C**

what's important

- ■ **Recognizing Middle C for either hand**
- ■ **Understanding that any finger can play Middle C**

let's get started

1 Middle C is the short line between the treble and bass staves. (Show the sample in the book.)

2 Any finger can play Middle C. Tickle Middle C with your RH finger 2, finger 4… Your LH finger 3, thumb…

3 Let's point to the notes and count: 1, 1, 1-2, 1, 1, 1-2 …

4 Watch how I change my fingers. (Play the piece, showing how the fingers change.)

5 It's your turn to try the piece and change your fingers. (If the student's rounded hand shape flattens, have him or her brace fingers 2 and 3 with the thumb.)

Middle C is in the middle of the grand staff, not the middle of the keyboard.

THE STAFF

Duet Appendix pp. 174-175   CD Tracks 32-33
8-measure IMPROVISATION at the end.
Students create their own "fancy" rhythms
using only Middle C.

explore & create

■ **Finger Tricks**
Start each hand with finger 2.

■ **Take a Dare**
Start each hand with finger 3!

■ **Disappearing Act**
Begin each line forte, then get softer to
the end.

■ **As You C It!**
Choose your own fingers and rhythms. Use
either hand. Make your own C music. I'll start
a duet part. Feel the beat and join me when
you're ready.

(See Video and Duet Appendix pp. 174-175)

partner pages

Sightreading
pp. 6-11

pedagogy pointers

The first piece that uses staff notation shows the
Grand Staff, with Middle C placed between the
staves. Both hands play this piece, making the
student aware that the hands "share" Middle C.
Each hand changes fingers on Middle C, so the
student does not think of it as the "thumb note".
The dynamics begin piano, then increase to forte
in each hand.

Improvisation is easy when the student plays one
note. Use this as a time to explore rhythm—don't
waste a minute letting your beginner create at the
keyboard.

 Any finger can play Middle C!

PIANO ADVENTURES VIDEO

see it in action

Teaching Video 31

Checking how to read and count the notes prepares
Hannah for this solid little march in which the
fingers switch with rhythmic regularity. Everything
about Hannah shows she's ready. She even sets her
own tempo before playing!

Not only do the fingers change, but so do the
dynamics, making this duet a colorful, as well as a
peppy, parade. Hannah's own march takes off with
syncopations and daredevil finger changes. And
what a natural, musical ending—on the fifth finger,
no less!

Ask Yourself

■ What does the teacher do when she presents the
piece?

■ What does the teacher do when Hannah plays the
piece the first time?

75

A Ten-Second Song

Lesson Book page 37

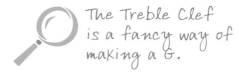

what's new

- **Treble G**
- **Two reading Guide Notes**

what's important

- **Understanding the Treble Clef**
- **Tracing the G Line**
- **Feeling the C-G hand shape**

let's get started

1 (Trace several large treble clefs.) What do we call this sign?

2 There's a secret to this sign. (Trace the G that's part of the treble clef.) It uses the letter G. We can call it the G clef. (Trace some Gs.)

3 When the G clef is on the staff, it circles the second line, the G line.

4 Trace the G line through this piece.

5 Which measures have only Middle Cs? Which measure has only Treble Gs? Which measure has both Middle Cs and Treble Gs?

6 Let's try the hand-shape exercise at the top of the page.

explore & create

- **Ten Seconds or Bust**
  Can we really play this piece in 10 seconds? What would we have to do? (Set a faster tempo with the duet.) Here we go!

- **Shazam—Two Hands**
  Let's try the piece with two hands, a little slowly first. Can we play it in 10 seconds with two hands?

- **You Copy Me**
  Get your RH ready over Middle C and Treble G. Close your eyes! See if you can copy what I play. (Play short examples using these two notes.)

- **I'll Copy You**
  Now I'll close my eyes and you be the leader!

The Treble Clef is a fancy way of making a G.

partner pages

Theory
p. 21 A Twenty-Second Royal Song

■ This page presents a variety of activities using Middle C and Treble G. First, students draw Middle C and Treble G on the Grand Staff. Next, students name the notes for the royal song "inside each clock". Lastly, students create a twenty-second piece by improvising an ending using Middle C and Treble G notes—all to a majestic, royal-sounding teacher duet.

pedagogy pointers

The Treble Clef is a fancy way of making a G. That's why it's also called the G Clef. This piece uses Middle C and Treble G, the two notes presented on the staff thus far. Playing these notes with the thumb and fifth finger opens up the hand.

Make drawing the treble clef a real accomplishment. Try drawing with different color markers and have the student circle which is best.

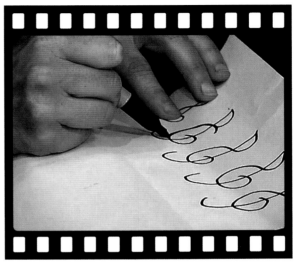

PIANO ADVENTURES VIDEO

see it in action

Teaching Video 32

Hannah traces some Gs over sample Treble Clefs, then learns that on the staff the Treble Clef circles around the second line. Tracing the G line through the piece reminds her where G is. When her thumb and fifth finger are ready over the keys, she's all set to play a piece that uses only Middle Cs and Treble Gs.

Now here comes the challenge—can she really make this a ten-second song? A speedy accompaniment sets the pace, and off she goes. What about another dare? Can she do it with both hands? After a cautious tryout, Hannah turns on the jets. Whaddaya know—a nine-second song!

Ask Yourself

■ What does Hannah's body language tell you?

4 UNIT

THE STAFF

Driving in the G Clef

Lesson Book page 38

what's new

- Playing two notes together in the same hand
- Building the arch by playing a fifth

what's important

- Playing a harmonic fifth with a good arch
- Playing a melodic fifth with a good arch

let's get started

1 We've got a traffic jam. Listen to the honking cars. (Demonstrate the fifth.)

2 Would you like to honk and beep this horn? (Have the student try some fifths.)

3 This is what it looks like when two notes play together. The notes are stacked up. (Show the sample on the page.)

4 Point to the notes while I play the piece.

5 I think you're ready to join the traffic jam. (Have the student try the piece.)

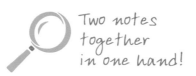

Two notes together in one hand!

explore & create

- **Transposition**
  You're in a new car—Model F. (Play the piece on F and C.)

- **More Transposition**
  Is that you in a convertible? (Play the piece on G and D.)

- **All Kinds of Horns**
  This highway is crowded. Let's make big semi truck honking sounds. (Model for the student and together play some low intervals and clusters.)

- Now let's make car honks in the middle range. (Together, play some intervals and clusters here.)

- How about a bicycle bell high on the keys? (Experiment together.)

- **The Robin and the Traffic Jam**
  Guess who's getting through the traffic jam—a little robin is walking right through. (Play some "little bird" music in the middle and have the student play sounds for the semi, the cars, or the bicycle.)

(See Video and Duet Appendix pp. 176-179)

Driving in the G Clef

Treble Clef = G Clef

The Treble Clef is also called the **G clef** because it circles around the G LINE on the staff.

The Treble or G clef came from the old letter G shown below.

Urgently
Play C and G together.
f Beep, beep, in the streets, beep, beep, traf - fic meets.

measure number 5
Cit - y sounds are all a - round, Beep, honk, beep!

Teacher Duet: (Student plays as written)
mf

38 ♩ CD 36-37 ✎ 22 ✑ 17 ♪ 12-15

FF1075

 Duet Appendix pp. 176-179   CD Tracks 36-37

partner pages

Theory
p. 22 The Treble Clef or G Clef

■ Treble clefs are fun to draw! Students draw a candy cane as a first step to drawing a treble clef. Tracing over the G line reinforces the G clef and location of the Treble G note.

Technique & Artistry
p. 17 The Great Cookie Chase

■ Playing a fifth reinforces a round hand shape and helps build the arch and outside of the hand.

■ Contrast the forte and piano measures. Drop firmly into the broken and blocked C-G fifth in measures 1-2.

■ Tell the student to play softly and close to the keys for measures 3-4. Steady quarter notes!

■ Ask the student, "Can you land on the next higher C without missing a beat? I'm going to be a rolling pin and chase your cookie up the keyboard. Don't let me catch you!"

Sightreading
pp. 12-15

pedagogy pointers

This is the first time the student plays two notes together in one hand. Playing a harmonic fifth is a natural way to build the arch in the hand.

The piece also reinforces the use of Treble G and its association with the G Clef. "Honking" encourages the student to play with a firm, loud tone.

PIANO ADVENTURES VIDEO

see it in action

Teaching Video 33

It's always a thrill to play notes together in one hand, and a fifth is a good "honking" and "beeping" sound. Patrick is eager to beep the horn (harmonic fifths) and move through the traffic (melodic fifths). The idea of driving steadily even though semis are sounding their own horns is a satisfying challenge.

But this highway's crowded. In addition to semis, there are other cars, even bicycles. What fun it is to explore all these sounds in different ranges of the keyboard while the perky little robin makes his way through the congestion. This is a crazy and exciting "traffic jam session"!

Ask Yourself

■ Describe the ways that Patrick is involved in learning and playing this piece. Which does he enjoy the most?

THE STAFF

Best Friends

Lesson Book page 39

what's new

- **Playing a fifth using both hands**
- **Any finger can play on any key**

what's important

- **Playing harmonic and melodic fifths using both hands**
- **Understanding that any finger can play on any key**

let's get started

1 Play your LH thumb on C. Now change to finger 2, then 3.

2 Play your RH thumb on C. Change to finger 2, then 3.

3 Check the piece. Which fingers should play C and G? You're ready!

4 Since your hands are best friends, this time they'll share playing C-G. Put your hands in your lap. Find the starting keys. Good! Let's try it again. (Repeat until automatic.)

5 How should we play the first line, loud or soft? What about the second line?

explore & create

- **New Friends**
  Play the piece using both second fingers. Feel your fingertips.

- **A Pair of Shorter Friends**
  Play the piece using both thumbs.

- **Choose Your Friends**
  Play the piece with any fingers you'd like!

- **Friends in New Neighborhoods**
  Visit the D-A neighborhood to make more new friends. Choose your fingers! Try the E-B neighborhood with any fingers. You've got a big social life!

80

partner pages

Theory
p. 23 Sightreading

- Are you ready for Eye-Training? Students shade the matching measures and follow three basic tips to sightread with just two notes—but notice the *f*, *mf*, and *p* signs!

- Time for Ear-Training
  Choose one measure to play from each line of music. The student listens closely and circles the measure heard.

Performance
p. 12 Chimes

- Brace finger 3 with the thumb for a firm fingertip.

- Ask the student which technique secret will help them drop with a forte sound into the keys.

- Will you use more or less arm weight at measure 5?

- Let's play with the duet. For the whole notes, can you pulse beats 2, 3, and 4 with a small up-and-down motion of your wrists? (Demonstrate)

pedagogy pointers

Here both hands share in playing harmonic and melodic fifths. Once again, the student should be reminded that any fingers, in either hand, could play these notes. But no matter which fingers play, the hand must be round, the fingers firm, and the shoulders relaxed.

Any finger can play on any key!

PIANO ADVENTURES VIDEO

see it in action

Teaching Video 34

Testing out several fingerings before playing the piece shows Patrick that any fingers can play these keys. Using the third fingers, though, makes it easy to drop into the keys with arm weight.

During the first read-through, his eyes stay on the music. He trusts his hands even when he makes a tiny mistake! And the words matter, as Patrick shows. It doesn't take long to achieve a steady performance, complete with an echo.

You can see those wheels turning when he gets to choose his own fingering. Wouldn't you know it would be the pinkies!

Ask Yourself

- Is there a particular moment that Patrick especially trusts his hands?

- How does the teacher remain involved in all of Patrick's performances?

Gorilla in the Tree

Lesson Book page 40

THE STAFF

what's new

- Bass F

what's important

- Recognizing Bass F on the staff
- Building the LH arch playing melodic fifths

let's get started

1 Let's warm up. (Place student's hand over Bass F and Middle C. Demonstrate how to rock back and forth.)

2 I'll play some short rhythmic patterns, like C-C-F. (Demonstrate) You copy me.

3 Now you make up some patterns, and I'll copy you.

4 (Show how Bass F sits on the fourth line, or second line going down.) Would you circle all the Bass Fs in this piece?

5 Let's see if the gorilla can swing from branch to branch. (Play the piece.)

The Bass Clef can also be called the F Clef!

explore & create

- **600 Pound Gorilla**
  What if this gorilla invited one of his bigger friends to swing with him? How would a 600 lb. gorilla sound? (Play the accompaniment slower and heavier.)

  (See Video)

- **800 Pound Gorilla**
  (Knock on the side of the piano.) Who's there? An 800 lb. gorilla! (Play the accompaniment even more slowly and loudly.)

- **The Gorilla Gang**
  More gorillas are coming to play. How do you think their music would sound? Can you play with two hands?

- **Jungle Dance**
  You play the drums, and I'll play the flute. (Show the student how to play a short drum pattern using F-C. Your flute melody could use the F Lydian mode [B-natural].)

 CD Tracks 40-41
4-measure IMPROVISATION at the end.
Students create their own gorilla tune using
Middle C and Bass F.

partner pages

Technique & Artistry
p. 17 Left-Hand Cookie Cutter

- Playing LH fifths to reinforce F-C keys, rounded hand shape, and arm weight parallels The Great Cookie Chase for RH.

- Coach the student to contrast f or p with heavier and lighter arm weight.

- Ask student, "Can you land on the next lower C without missing a beat?"

- Playing an octave higher, model a good hand shape and encourage the student to move quickly down the keys!

Sightreading
pp. 16-21

pedagogy pointers

Attention now shifts to the left hand and the Bass Clef. Learning Bass F on the staff extends the reading range. Having the student copy short patterns before learning a piece prepares the student for the technique that will be needed to play it. Reading then becomes easier and more fluent because the fingers are ready.

Simple two-note pieces are ideal for exploring the keyboard range, discovering dynamics and tone, and playing hands together.

PIANO ADVENTURES VIDEO

see it in action

Teaching Video 35

The patterns using the new note, Bass F, are a good warm-up, and circling the note in the score reinforces the placement of the note on the staff. This gorilla is ready to rock. Here come the bananas!

Who's that rapping? More gorillas? Hannah's playing gets heavier and slower—and more secure—as gorilla friends come to visit. The accompaniment sets the tempo and mood, and Hannah responds. The giant gorilla requires two hands!

Ask Yourself

- What's especially interesting about Hannah's original patterns?

- What does Hannah check before she plays the piece for the first time?

- How does the teacher change the accompaniments as the gorillas get heavier?

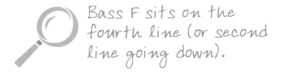 Bass F sits on the fourth line (or second line going down).

83

My Invention

Lesson Book page 41

what's new

- ■ Open "space" sounds

what's important

- ■ Reinforcing Middle C, Treble G, and Bass F
- ■ Pushing off the third finger on Bass F with energy that comes from the shoulder

explore & create

- ■ **New Inventions**
  Play the LH one octave lower, or the RH one octave higher.

- ■ **My Invention Is Expanding**
  How far apart can you put your hands and still play the piece?

- ■ **Command Your Invention**
  If you had an invention, what would you like it to do? Clean your room? Make chocolate?

- ■ **The Popsicle Invention**
  An 11-year-old boy invented the popsicle. Find out how he did it at kidzworld.com/site/p1010.htm

- ■ **Play a Real Invention**
  Benjamin Franklin invented a glass armonica. You can play it online at fi.edu/franklin/musician/musician.html Click on Play a Tune.

let's get started

1 Let's discover which notes are in the "invention box" (See the picture.) The LH gets to play the new Bass F.

2 Test all your fingers on Bass F. Which feels the most comfortable? Which finger does this piece use?

3 How does this invention "work"? Which measures are the same? Which are different?

4 Where does the RH play two notes together—like Driving in the G Clef?

partner pages

Theory
pp. 24-25 The Bass Clef or F Clef
The Greatest Gadget

- Students learn to draw a bass clef, trace the F line, and choose to draw a bass or treble clef to match each picture.

- Students name the notes (Bass F, Middle C, or Treble G) to complete an inventive story called "The Greatest Gadget".

Performance
p. 13 Listen to the Drums

- Tap the rhythm on a drum with the correct hands. Tapping the dynamics on Mm. 5-6 will give a natural pulse to this 4/4 piece.

- Play on balanced finger 3s. Use arm weight to drop into Middle C and Bass F.

- Play again, using finger 2s on Middle C and Bass F.

- Play with the duet at three tempos:

  - a slow processional march

  - a moderate drum call for the villagers to gather together

  - a fast, energetic dance by the firelight

Sightreading
pp. 22-25

pedagogy pointers

My Invention combines and reinforces Middle C, Treble G, and Bass F. Bass F, however, is the only note played by the left hand. The left hand can push off on the third finger, making it easy for the student to play from the shoulder. The right hand plays both melodic and harmonic fifths, much like in Driving in the G Clef.

Comparing measures to see what's the same and what's different is the best way to help a student read a new piece. Looking ahead and checking for patterns also teaches the student how music is put together.

PIANO ADVENTURES VIDEO

see it in action

Teaching Video 36

This "invention" stretches Philip's imagination and opens his ears to new sounds. Bass F, the new note, gets a workout. Any finger can play it, but Philip sees why this piece uses the third finger. Bracing that finger can help to make bombastic sounds.

Creative repetition frees Philip to explore the range of the keyboard and to experiment with different tempos. The "weird" gears come to life in the mechanical-sounding duet. Philip's facial and physical reactions show that he's anything but a "robot" as he digs into that last solemn performance!

Ask Yourself

- What does Philip do when the teacher demonstrates the piece?

- As Philip's invention gets further and further apart, does anything change in his body language?

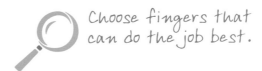

Choose fingers that can do the job best.

85

Note Names & Interval Contour

**Musicians read note names and the interval contour.
Both skills combine for musical fluency.**

Recognizing Note Names

■ Provides keyboard orientation

■ Promotes confidence

■ Frees attention for musicality

■ Establishes musical literacy

*But reading by note name alone often leads to
unmusical, note-by-note decoding.*

Up or Down?

Ask: Which direction? Up, down, or same?

The interval of a second *(step)* and the interval
of a third *(skip)* are so prominent in music that
we easily focus only on steps, skips, and repeated
notes at the Primer Level.

Reading by Intervallic Contour

■ Promotes expressive, musical shaping

■ Expands perception to several notes at once

■ Engages pattern recognition

■ Invites fluid eye-tracking

*But reading by interval without note recognition
may lead to disorientation, inaccuracy, or
embarrassment.*

Step or Skip?

Then ask: Are the notes stepping or skipping?

Which is more
important,
naming notes
or reading
intervals?

Both are
necessary.

Group lesson—3:30pm

Note Naming

Most teachers have seen piano students equate notes with finger numbers. This is no surprise considering that most methods teach notes using a fixed, preset hand position.

In Piano Adventures, fingerings are varied when new notes are introduced. For example, Middle C March is played with fingers 1, 2, and 3, not just with the thumb. Treble G is played as frequently with finger 3 as with finger 5. Bass F is handled similarly in My Invention and The Dance Band. The student learns that a note's position on the staff indicates a particular key (or pitch), not a particular finger.

Steps and Skips

The typical Primer student relates better to the terms *step* and *skip* than second and third because these terms describe the actual motion:

Stepping up or down …
　　　to the very next key
　　　to the very next finger
　　　to the next letter name

Similarly for skips …
　　　skip a key
　　　skip a finger
　　　skip a letter name

These aspects of *steps* are addressed in the pre-reading pages with C-D-E-F-G March (Lesson Book p. 28). The student *hears*, *feels*, and *sees* the stepwise motion while learning adjacent letter names and assimilating the mirror image fingerings between the right and left hands.

Reading Steps and Skips

On page 42, after orientation to the staff with the notes Middle C, Treble G, and Bass F, the student is presented with a set of three notes—D, E, F—all at once. While we expect the student to learn these note names over the next several weeks, the immediate aim is to read by note contour. Thus, the page is paired with Mister Bluebird which introduces stepwise motion on the staff (LINE to the next SPACE, or SPACE to the next LINE).

Notice how Mister Bluebird seeks the integration of individual note recognition and reading by intervallic contour. The Discovery Question asks the student to name each note, and the questions above each measure ask whether the notes are stepping up, stepping down, or repeating.

Page 52 introduces *skips* on the staff, first as LINE to LINE, then later on page 54 as SPACE to SPACE. The student needs time to imprint each of these visual patterns.

MIDDLE C - D - E - F - G

March on D-E-F

Lesson Book page 42

what's new

- Treble notes D-E-F

what's important

- Reading treble D-E-F
- Reinforcing the concept of line and space notes
- Playing with a round hand shape

let's get started

1 On the piano, three white keys come between Middle C and Treble G. Can you name them? (Refer to the example in the book.) This is how we write them on the staff. Which are space notes?

2 Let's play these notes a few times. Use fingers 2-3-4. I'll play a duet.

(See Video and Duet Appendix p. 180)

3 Circle all the notes that repeat.

4 Look at measures 1 and 2. Are there any other measures that look like that? Is there any difference between them at all? (*f* and *p*)

5 Start the dwarfs marching.

Melodies can begin or end on any finger.

explore & create

- **Ear Tunes**
  Place fingers 2-3-4 over Treble D-E-F. Close your eyes! I'll play some short patterns. See if you can copy me.

  (See Video)

- **D-E-F Ostinato**
  Play D-E-F over and over again, feeling the beat. I'll play a melody above. Can you keep your steady beat?

  (See Video and Duet Appendix p. 180)

- **Pixie March**
  Play the piece high on the keyboard, softly and quickly. Maybe the pixies march on tiptoes!

- **Dorian Dwarfs**
  (Show the student a few patterns that could be played using all five fingers over C-D-E-F-G, but beginning and ending on D [Dorian Mode].) Make up your own dwarf march over my duet!

  (See Video and Duet Appendix p. 181)

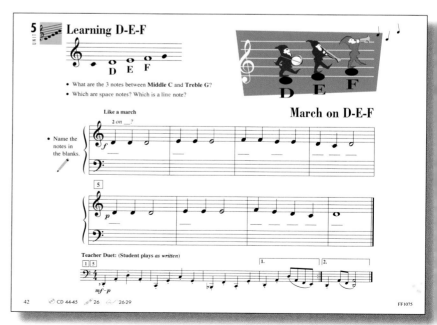

partner pages

Theory
p. 26 D-E-F in the Treble Clef

■ Students draw D, E, and F on the staff and then connect D-E-F notes to the matching "elves at play" on the keyboard.

Sightreading
pp. 26-29

pedagogy pointers

This piece fills in the notes between Middle C and Treble G and gives each of them special attention by repeating them in a well-known rhythm pattern. This is also a good chance to reinforce the concept of line and space notes.

Although the right-hand fingers cover the keys from C to G, the emphasis on the middle fingers creates a melody in the Dorian Mode. The student not only has a new musical experience, but discovers that melodies do not always begin or end on the thumb note.

The early reading pieces on the staff are the perfect opportunity to continue exploring improvisation. The student is able to take a break from the demands of visual focus and change to the stimulation of aural focus. And you'll both have fun in the process!

Music à la mode—
the Dorian Mode!

PIANO ADVENTURES VIDEO

see it in action

Teaching Video 37

Playing and reading the new notes gets Hannah's fingers ready, but also "tunes" her in to the sound of the Dorian Mode. Those elfin horns inspire her to follow them to a gentle ending.

Circling all the repeated notes makes her aware of what will happen in the piece. Reading it through then becomes easy. The duet sets the mood for the marching elves.

A few Dorian "seeds" (motifs) are "planted" and Hannah is ready to improvise. Although she's cautious at first, the eighth notes and rhythms she hears in the teacher's part loosen her own fingers. These Dorian dwarfs are perky fellows!

Ask Yourself

■ What is happening when Hannah circles the notes?

■ What type of rhythmic and melodic patterns does the teacher model before the final improvisation?

Mister Bluebird

Lesson Book page 43

what's new

- ■ Stepwise motion on the staff
- ■ Line-space; space-line

what's important

- ■ Directional reading
- ■ Melodic contour

explore & create

- ■ **Play Where I Point**
  This is a game to train your eyes. (Playfully zoom your index finger only to first notes in different measures. Then point to third beats.)

- ■ **Repeat What I Play**
  I'll play a few notes in the C five-finger scale. Repeat what I play. (Assess how easily the student is able to copy.)

- ■ **Same Game, Eyes Closed**
  Place your hand in the C five-finger scale. Then with your eyes closed, listen for the sound stepping up or down. (Play one octave lower.)

- ■ **You've Got the Power**
  Now you be the leader. See if I can hear with my eyes closed.

- ■ **Silly Bluebird**
  The lyrics say, "The Bluebird practices all day long". In his practice, let's have him play a wrong note for the final C.

  (See Video)

let's get started

1 (If you can, use a staircase to introduce stepping up and down.)

2 Lines and spaces on the staff are like stair steps for notes to go up and down.

3 Let's trace the way the notes move in the piece. (Use the student's arm, an imitation bird, or actual stair steps.)

(See Video)

4 On which note does the Bluebird start his song? Now watch how he goes down and up. Eyes on the music!

(Duet Appendix pp. 182-183)

When notes move from line to space on the staff, they either step up or down.

 Duet Appendix pp. 182-183

 CD Tracks 46-47
8-measure IMPROVISATION at the end. Students create their own bluebird tune using the C five-finger scale.

partner pages

Theory
p. 27 Steps on the Staff

■ Students connect the two-note "bird calls" that STEP UP to the bluebird house and the ones that STEP DOWN to the cherries on the ground. The next step is to name and play the notes. Can you sing the bluebird's "tur-ee" as you play?

pedagogy pointers

Attention here is on recognizing stepwise motion (line-space-line) and note names on the staff from Middle C to Treble G. With the exception of measures 7 and 8, the directional movement is clearly down and up.

Although the emphasis should be on reading directionally, the student should also be aware of the note names. All the notes in the C five-finger scale are played from top to bottom, but this position is not yet named as such—another example of the experience preceding the definition.

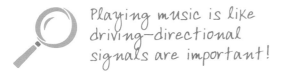 *Playing music is like driving—directional signals are important!*

PIANO ADVENTURES VIDEO

see it in action

Teaching Video 38

Philip's Bluebird traces the direction of the notes in the piece—first vertically down and up, then as down, up, and repeat move across the keys. Playing the piece on a small set of tuned bars relates stepwise motion to keys. Stepping down and up from Treble G and Middle C reinforces these notes and uses all the right-hand fingers in turn.

When the Bluebird doesn't practice, he might get the last note wrong, and Philip has fun exploring some possible "wrong" notes. What a crazy bird!

Ask Yourself

■ What guides Patrick's movements when he is tracing directions before playing?

■ What tells you that Patrick feels the rhythm?

MIDDLE C - D - E - F - G

The Dance Band

Lesson Book page 44

what's new

- Time signature
- 4/4 meter

what's important

- To understand 4/4 meter
- To recognize and respond to rhythm patterns
- To push off the LH third finger with energy

let's get started

1 Can you tell time on a clock? In music we "tell time", but in a different way. The 4/4 at the start of this piece is like a clock. (Explain 4/4 time signature.)

2 Would you like to be the drummer for The Dance Band? Let's tap the rhythm on the keyboard cover (or a drum). Use both hands. Then tap with your hands as they are used in the piece.

(See Video)

3 Can you point out three measures that step up D-E-F?

4 How many measures are the same? Try them out.

5 Look carefully. Can you find a C five-finger scale that steps down?

6 Is your dance band ready to roll?

explore & create

- **Time Puzzle**
  (Write several measures of notes in 4/4 time, without bar lines.) Can you add bar lines to measure the time? What tells you you're at the end?

- **Your Own Time Puzzles**
  Make up some time puzzles for me.

- **Fun on One**
  This band has rhythm! Can you stamp and clap on all the count 1s (downbeats)?

- **Kick It Up**
  Let's get this band rockin'. Pick your speed and turn up the amps!

(See Video)

 4/4 meter implies an impulse on the downbeat.

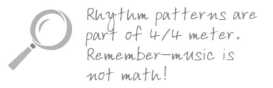

Rhythm patterns are part of 4/4 meter. Remember—music is not math!

partner pages

Theory
p. 28 Conga Line Rhythms

- Students explore the 4/4 time signature by drawing bar lines and completing measures correctly.

Technique & Artistry
p. 18 Dance Band Drummer

- This exercise promotes a changing RH position, shifting the hand up stepwise.

- To prepare, have the student brace RH 3 with the thumb and shift from Middle C to D, to E, and to F.

- Circle this rhythm pattern three times in the piece:

- Drop into Bass F with a braced finger 3 on the downbeat. What technique secrets are you using?

Performance
p. 14 Classical March p. 15 Rex, the Tyrannosaurus

- For Classical March, review the notes of the C five-finger scale with a step-and-repeat pattern.

- Rex, the Tyrannosaurus opens with the three guide notes (Middle C, Treble G, and Bass F) followed by a stepwise marching melody.

Sightreading
pp. 30-33

pedagogy pointers

Playing in 4/4 meter has already been experienced in many pieces, and rhythm patterns common to this meter have also become part of the student's rhythm "vocabulary". The step taken here is to identify 4/4 meter and explain what a time signature does. At this point it makes sense to count 1-2-3-4, but you could still revert to counting "1" for each quarter, "1-2" for each half note, and so on, or use this type of counting as an alternate.

Once again, as in My Invention, the left hand plays only Bass F. Here is another chance to have the left-hand third finger spring off the key to set the downbeat and to release weight from the shoulder.

PIANO ADVENTURES VIDEO

see it in action

Teaching Video 39

Playing and using rhythm patterns in 4/4 makes it easy to introduce time signature as a way to express measured counting.

By tapping on the downbeat and clapping on the remaining beats Patrick begins to sense the accented and unaccented aspects of meter, especially when this activity is combined with singing familiar melodies.

Tapping the rhythm for The Dance Band transfers the concept of 4/4 meter to a piece. By tapping softer and faster Philip hears and feels rhythmic patterns, not just single pulses.

Learning to tap on the off-beats happens naturally, without fuss or explanation. This slyly introduces syncopation—emphasis on the off-beats—that is so much a part of the jazz idiom.

Philip discovers how to learn a piece by checking what's the same and what's different. His dance band really rocks with energy. Faster!

Ask Yourself

- How does the teacher "fix" Philip's first rhythm inaccuracies?

- Has Philip internalized the meter and rhythm pattern? How do you know?

Frogs on Logs

Lesson Book page 45

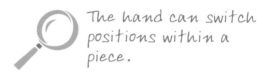

what's new

- **Change of hand position within the piece**

what's important

- **Moving finger 2 to three different positions within the piece**
- **Noting the finger numbers on the page**

explore & create

- **Mighty Low Bullfrog Splash**
  How big is your bullfrog's splash? Play the final LH note on the lowest C.

- **Hopping Higher**
  Play the pattern in Mm. 1-2, but keep hopping to the next key until you get to C an octave higher.

- **Frisky Frog Improvisation**
  Let's explore keyboard ribbit sounds. Play steps with fingers separately or together. Now listen as I create a frog song for you. A low "ribbit" will end my piece. Will you create a frisky frog song for me? (See Video)

The hand can switch positions within a piece.

let's get started

1 What do frogs like to do? (Jump) Put your second finger on C. Make it hop to D. Hop to E. Hop back to C.

2 Let's circle all the repeated notes in this piece. These frogs are really hopping, aren't they?

3 Watch me play and sing this piece. Fourteen little frogs (hop to D). Sat upon a log (hop to E).

(See Video)

4 Now your fingers can try out the hops.

5 At the very end, your left hand can jump onto Middle C. (Use the LH braced finger 3 to play the final C.)

A fingering pattern might also be a rhythm pattern.

CD Tracks 50-51
4-measure IMPROVISATION at the end.
Students create frog sounds by freely
hopping around to any white or black keys.

partner pages

Theory
p. 29 Risky Rhythms / Asleep on the Lily Pads

■ Eye-Training requires students to circle incorrect 4/4 measures.

■ Ear-Training offers a "frog lullaby" improvisation using the C five-finger scale with duet.

Technique & Artistry
p. 19 Finger Hops

■ This little technique pattern "hops up" the keys from C to C.

■ Students should memorize this exercise and watch their hands to check for firm fingertips.

■ Once the pattern is learned, alternate from *f* to *p* for each hand shift. The teacher may model the sound an octave lower.

■ Try variations using fingers 1-2 or 3-4.

Performance
p. 16 The Inchworm

■ We've been doing "frog hops" on the keys. Now let's try a creeping inchworm pattern.

■ First we creep slowly up and down. (Demonstrate Mm. 1-2.)

■ Then the inchworm scrunches up to D and does the pattern again. (Continue)

■ For the last C, play any lower C with finger 2 or 3 braced with the thumb.

Sightreading
pp. 34-37

pedagogy pointers

This is the first piece in which the hand changes position within the piece. Since the middle fingers are used throughout the piece, the hand can remain in balance as it hops from key to key. This also encourages a drop from the shoulder at the beginning of each position change.

PIANO ADVENTURES VIDEO

see it in action

Teaching Video 40

Jumping frogs might land in different places. The first test of finger 2 moving to other keys sets up the action. By circling the repeated notes, Vivian sees that these frogs are really hopping!

After she learns the pattern in the first four measures, Vivian is ready to go. A big left-hand bullfrog jumps into the pond on the last C.

Then the frogs have a free-for-all, hopping on seconds wherever they'd like to go, using either or both hands. The big, fat bullfrog signals the end of the scamper. Frisky frogs!

Ask Yourself

■ What does the teacher do when Vivian circles the repeated notes?

■ What's the advantage of the left-hand "bullfrog" landing on a braced finger?

Sightreading Secret—Patterns!

In language reading, single letters are perceived in chunks— as words which combine into meaningful phrases. Similarly, for fluent music reading, notes must be perceived in chunks as rhythmic and tonal patterns which give musical meaning.

Recognizing note names and rhythmic values becomes truly beneficial when a student understands how these "facts" form larger and related "wholes". These "wholes" (patterns) become building blocks which form increasingly bigger "wholes". Reading in *patterns* is the key to sightreading.

Help Yourself to a Chunk!

Cognitive psychologists like to call such wholes and patterns "chunks".

An interval is a very small *chunk*.

Not two single notes D and E, but the interval of a *step*.

Not just C to E, but the interval of a *skip*.

Two have been reduced to one.

Chord recognition at later levels will reduce three notes to one—a triad. Recognition of tonic and dominant notes and harmonies similarly gives meaning and context.

Reading Challenge 1

All this sounds rather complex for the Primer Level. Indeed, a student's capacity to perceive patterns will improve with exposure to more music theory during the course of Piano Adventures®. So what patterns are we looking for at this early level?

In earlier pages we discussed the importance of reading by *intervallic contour* in addition to individual note recognition. At the Primer Level, this perception of intervallic contour is the first step in pattern recognition.

Do the notes **step** up, *down*, or *repeat?*

Scan the shape of the note movement to find a visual pattern with aural meaning.

The first Primer Level reading challenge focuses only on stepwise motion. This helps the student concentrate on contour patterns.

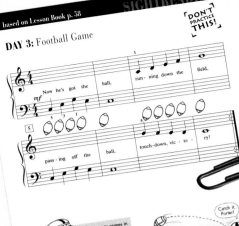

Reading Challenge 2

The next reading challenge—and also technical challenge—is to perceive patterns with **skips**. The visual cue is *line-to-line* and *space-to-space*. The technical, tactile cue is to skip a finger.

Note that the Primer Level focuses first only on line-to-line recognition, then only on space-to-space. We're building the student's capacity to instantly perceive the pattern!

Turbo-Charged Reading— "Chunking"

For accelerated reading skill, the excellent reader detects not only notes and intervals, but groupings of notes that form *familiar* patterns—melodic, harmonic, and rhythmic.

At the Primer Level, we work on chunking simple rhythmic patterns. Each rhythm pattern is a group of note values—a rhythmic "chunk". It is important to repeatedly see and hear these rhythm patterns so they become very familiar.

Some examples:

 or

Three notes become one pattern. Four notes become one pattern.

This entire rhythm can be chunked into patterns:

Chunk	Same Chunk	Same Chunk	New

Now there are really just two rhythmic patterns!

The Primer Level Sightreading Book

There are many, many patterns—even at the Primer Level. How do the many notes become recognizable as patterns? Through repeated exposure!

The Piano Adventures® Sightreading Book repeatedly exposes the student to familiar patterns by presenting variations on the Primer Lesson Book pieces.

Encountering the same pattern over and over in these variations, the student eventually perceives in chunks. This frees attention for other visual, aural, and tactile perceptions!

Begin exposing Primer students to sightreading from their earliest lessons and watch their sightreading "muscles" develop.

Most of all, remember that recognizing patterns is a powerhouse tool. Spot the unfamiliar against a backdrop of the familiar—that's a winning secret!

The Primer Sightreading Book includes educational art. Little Treble, Little Bass, Penny Piano, Freddie Forte, Buddy Barline, and other characters emphasize reading basics while encouraging the student through 96 pages of sightreading.

Let's Play Ball!

Lesson Book page 46

what's new

■ B below Middle C

what's important

■ Recognizing B below Middle C

■ Good distinctions between half and quarter notes

let's get started

1 What key is just below Middle C on the piano? (B) Let's play back and forth from Middle C and B with LH fingers 1-2. I'll play a duet.

(Duet Appendix p. 184)

2 On the staff, B is the space note right below Middle C. (Show the example on the page.)

3 Circle all the Bs in the piece.

4 On which note does your RH begin? On what finger?

5 Here's a twisty pattern that you'll need to wind up in order to throw your ball. (Isolate Mm. 5 and 6 and "wind these up" a few times.)

6 Batter up. Let's play ball!

(Duet Appendix p. 185)

explore & create

■ **Pitch Out**
When you finish the piece, throw a hard fast-ball with your RH and catch it with your LH. Get that runner out!

■ **Teammates**
(Show another student how to play a simple duet. [RH] C C [LH] G G: steady quarter notes.)

■ **Scouting for New Players**
(Show another student how to play a drum accompaniment:

Then you'll have a trio: the duet plus the drum part.)

♪♫ Duet Appendix pp. 184-185   CD Tracks 52-53

partner pages

Theory
p. 30 Learning Bass Clef B

- Draw the new Bass Clef B and review drawing Treble G, Middle C, and Bass Clef F.

- Shade the baseballs with Bass Clef Bs and count up the total.

- Lastly, count the Bass Clef Bs in each melody and sightread the examples.

Performance
p. 17 Cowboy Joe

- New Bass Clef note B is approached stepwise from Middle C to begin the song.

- Cowboy Joe has a technique secret. Can you guess which one he uses for his thumbs?

- Where do Mm. 1-2 repeat? For fun, have the student play this pattern with eyes closed?

- What is the only difference between Mm. 3-4 and Mm. 7-8?

- Ask the student to play the last C with a braced LH finger 2. Pretend it's a lasso!

Sightreading
pp. 38-41

pedagogy pointers

We now begin with recognition of notes on the bass staff. In this piece B below Middle C is featured as a step down from Middle C and also as part of a leap from treble G to B. There is further reinforcement to distinguish quarter from half notes. It's a good idea to prepare the "wind-up" melodic and finger pattern in measures 5-7 before presenting the entire piece.

PIANO ADVENTURES VIDEO

see it in action

Teaching Video 41

The "wind-up" in measures 5 and 6 is practiced by rote as a finger warm-up. It's like running from third base to first and back. David can even do this with his eyes closed! As he then discovers, using this pattern in the piece is easy, especially as the prelude to the leap in measure 7. No wonder he doesn't need to look down to find the B.

When Patrick and Philip join the team, they're poised to play the piece as teammates. And they're also ready to throw the runner out and save the game. Let's play ball!

Ask Yourself

- Is there any purpose beside fun in throwing and catching that ball?

- Could this be a recital idea?

A finger warm-up can make reading a new piece easy.

Petite Minuet

Lesson Book page 47

what's new

- **3/4 time signature**
- **Minuet**

what's important

- **Feeling the flow in triple meter**
- **Understanding 3/4 time signature**
- **Feeling and recognizing a new rhythmic pattern**

let's get started

1 This couple (point to the picture) is doing a minuet, a graceful, old court dance that's always in 3/4 time.

2 While I play some famous minuets, you play dotted half notes on high Gs. Use both hands with braced finger 3s. Feel the three beats. (See Video and Duet Appendix pp. 186-187)

3 Let's tap this rhythm (Mm. 1-2):
Min-u-et curt-sy. Min-u-et bow-ing.

4 Here's how this rhythm pattern looks in the music. Find and circle other patterns like this in the piece.

5 On which note does your LH begin? How about your RH? Your hands are ready to dance the minuet!

explore & create

- **What a Trill!**
On the last C, your LH can play a short trill (Demonstrate). Musicians often added a trill decoration to the minuet.

- **Minuet Rhythms**
(Write four measures of notes in 3/4 time.) Let's tap these rhythms (or play rhythm instruments). Here are four more measures. Let's tap! Now, you tap rhythm one and I'll tap rhythm two. Feel the beat!

- **Wigs and Wide Skirts**
(Describe, or show pictures, of how minuet dancers were dressed and why they moved carefully. Here's a chance to show students how to bow!)

 A 3/4 meter dances!

partner pages

Theory
p. 31 Tricky Time Signatures

■ For Eye-Training, students draw a 3/4 time signature, write a measure of 3/4 rhythm, and write the correct time signature for musical examples.

■ For Ear-Training, students listen and identify examples as in 4/4 or 3/4 time.

Performance
p. 18 Lullaby and Goodnight

■ What is the time signature? What does it mean?

■ Point out three measures that use the dotted half note.

■ The LH uses only one note. What is it?

■ Let's learn the second line first. Sing, F-up-down, E-up-down, D-down-down, C-2-3. Good! Let's play that three times since we're in 3/4 time!

■ Play the entire song. If it sounds slow and gentle like a lullaby, I might fall asleep at the end. (Pretend to fall asleep.)

pedagogy pointers

A minuet provides a natural introduction to 3/4 time. All triple meters contain a sense of flow as well as a leaning on the downbeat. Unless the tempo is quite slow, it's almost a feeling of one-to-the-bar. The minuet is not a familiar dance, but the words and illustration provide some clues.

Feeling the meter is more important than an explanation of it. Since the intention is to convey to the student something of the elegance of the dance, what better way than to use genuine minuets as models?

PIANO ADVENTURES VIDEO

see it in action

Teaching Video 42

You can almost picture Tatiana dressed for this court dance as she uses elegant braced fingers and flexible wrists to play downbeats while listening to Bach Minuets. This enables her to feel the new time signature, and it also models the spirit and style of a "minuet". As you can see, she's ready to keep on dancing!

Recognizing rhythmic patterns in 3/4 prepares her for fluent reading and for feeling the natural stress points in such patterns.

And how easy it is to lay some groundwork for Baroque ornamentation by tucking in a little trill on the last note. Tatiana is a good triller! This minuet deserves a special curtsy!

Ask Yourself

■ How would you describe Tatiana's response when she plays with the Bach minuets?

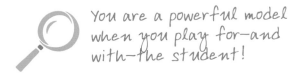

You are a powerful model when you play for—and with—the student!

Rodeo

Lesson Book page 48

what's new

- ■ **A is a line note**
- ■ **A is the top line on the bass staff**

what's important

- ■ **Recognizing A on the bass staff**
- ■ **Using familiar notes in the treble staff with varied fingering**

let's get started

1 Can you say the alphabet backwards from C?

2 (Point to the example at the top of the page.) Line-Space-Line. C-B-A.

3 Check out measures 1 and 2. Try it out. First down, then up.

4 Which RH finger plays G? What's the only note the RH plays in line two? Let's visit the rodeo!

A motive from a piece can become part of an improvisation.

explore & create

- ■ **A New Kind of Rodeo**
  Work at the piece in 2-measure sections.
  Play a two-measure introduction.
  Student answers playing Mm. 1-2.
  Play another two-measure introduction.
  Student answers playing Mm. 3-4.
  Continue this way through the piece.

  (See Video and Duet Appendix pp. 188-189)

- ■ **Slow Horse**
  What would an old, slow rodeo horse sound like? (Play Mm. 1-2 slowly as an introduction for the duet.)

- ■ **Faster Horses**
  Some horses run faster. Let's try a white horse who's a bit quicker. How about an even faster black horse? The race is on! Who's the winner?

  (See Video)

- ■ **Student Ostinato**
  Have the student play the first two measures as an ostinato, lower on the piano, and with two hands: Ro-de-o, Ro-de-o! (You improvise over the ostinato.)

  (See Video and Duet Appendix pp. 190-191)

partner pages

Theory
p. 32 "A", You Are Awesome

■ This page reinforces Bass Clef A and other notes learned. Students complete the Poem for a Rodeo Horse by naming and playing each note on the piano.

Technique & Artistry
p. 20 Walking the Thumb

■ Perching the thumb on the side tip controls wrist height and helps prevent a sagging wrist.

■ This sequential stepping pattern should be memorized so students may watch their thumb perch as they play.

■ The hand shifts allow students to "break out" of a stationary hand position. It also promotes thinking in patterns and quick memorization.

Sightreading
pp. 42-45

pedagogy pointers

The reading range in the left hand expands to A. It's easy to find by stepping down from Middle C. The many repeated notes in the piece provide a "bounce" for the rodeo. When the left hand is more active (measures 5-7), the right hand remains on G so the focus can be on the bass staff and the new note.

 Working in small sections shows the student how to practice.

PIANO ADVENTURES VIDEO

see it in action

Teaching Video 43

Ingrid finds A on the top line of the bass staff by saying the alphabet backwards from Middle C. That starts the rodeo. After her right hand puts finger 3 on G, the piece is ready. How easy to play the second line if the right hand only plays G.

It's fun to play two measures at a time following a two-measure introduction.

Some horses and broncos are slower, some are faster. The "blue" horse turns out to be the winner.

And then a magic way to use the new note! C-B-A becomes a two-hand "rodeo" ostinato low on the keyboard. When the teacher plays rockin' rodeo music over the ostinato, the race is on!

Ask Yourself

■ What does the teacher do with the accompaniments to convey tempo and mood?

■ What experiences does the ostinato/duet at the end offer the student?

MIDDLE C - B - A - G - F

Russian Folk Song

Lesson Book page 49

what's new

- Playing familiar notes at a quick tempo

what's important

- Checking which notes step up, step down, or repeat
- Checking which sections repeat
- Strong contrast between forte and piano

let's get started

1 Let's circle all the repeated notes in this piece. There are lots of them!

2 Try out measures 1-3. Compare these with measures 4-6. Another repeat—of a whole section!

3 B and A in the left hand are the only slow notes in the piece. What kind of rhythm is it?

4 Compare measures 10-12 with measures 7-9. More repeats!

5 What's different about these last two repeats? (Mm. 10-12 are an echo.)

explore & create

- **Varied Fingerings**
  A different Russian wants to lead off. Begin with RH finger 4.

- **All with One Hand**
  If finger 5 begins the right hand, you could play the piece with one hand! Try this out.

- **Fast Footsteps**
  All those repeated notes are feet stomping. To go faster, stay close to the keys. Play quickly with my duet.

- **Your Own Sailor Dance**
  Get set over A-B-C-D-E with RH fingers 1-2-3-4-5. Create your own sailor dance with the duet. (Elaborate on the duet to support the new dance.)

Directional reading is the key to success!

partner pages

Theory
p. 33 The Patterns of Russian Folk Song

■ This folk song has two main melody patterns. Copying the two patterns correctly on the Grand Staff continues to review concepts and develop reading awareness.

Performance
p. 19 The Opposite Song

■ The music alphabet steps up, A to G, then back down.

■ Bass F is the surprise note. Find it!

■ Change the title to The Opposite Song Is Long. Play the last two measures as a special ending in lower octaves.

pedagogy pointers

Good readers always watch the directions in which notes move, and they catch which parts are the same or different. In Russian Folk Song, the player must be very careful of the repeats and steps. Even though the left hand plays only a few notes, it must always be ready. The echoing phrases make this a good piece in which to emphasize the importance of dynamics.

Pieces such as this are also an opportunity to model notching up the tempo bit by bit with the teacher duet. In addition, teaching with imagery from the piece keeps the lesson alive, promotes repetition, and generates a higher level of performance.

 To play fast repeated notes, stay close to the keys.

PIANO ADVENTURES VIDEO

see it in action

Teaching Video 44

By circling the repeated notes, then comparing the measures and sections, Ingrid is forming good reading habits. And it's really easy to play when you're ready after having looked through the whole piece.

Those Russian sailors like to change their fingers. This keeps them from being locked into set positions, or thinking that certain fingers play only certain keys.

If the right-hand fifth finger begins, Ingrid discovers that she can play the piece with only one hand! It's no wonder those Russian sailors can stomp and dance up a storm—and end with such a gentlemanly bow.

Ask Yourself

■ What is happening when Ingrid circles the repeated notes?

■ What does the teacher do while Ingrid reads the piece?

Come See the Parade!

Lesson Book pages 50-51

what's new

- Bass staff—top space G
- The first 16-measure piece on the Grand Staff

what's important

- Recognizing and playing top space G on the bass staff
- Playing a longer piece that reviews many concepts

let's get started

1 Step down several times with your LH from Middle C to Bass G. Say the key names aloud. Does it sound like a march as you play?

2 Point to the notes at the top of the page and say, "Line-space-line-space". Notice that G is the top space.

3 Let's try measures 5 and 6. Find another place where you play the same thing.

4 The piano imitates horns for the introduction. Which two notes are used? Where do the horns return to end the piece?

explore & create

- **Out of Sight**
  The band disappears as it marches down the street at the end. How would this sound?

- **Come Join My Parade**
  Could other players join the parade? (With a partner, or as a group: Tap on a drum, table top, or triangle, march around the room, play an ostinato C-C-G-G on another piano.)

- **A Medley of Tunes**
  This band can play many songs! Combine a group of your favorites—like Driving in the G Clef, Mister Bluebird, A Ten-Second Song … (Play a vamp while finding the next page. Using sticky notes will help.) Begin and end with Come See the Parade!

(See Video and Duet Appendix pp. 192-193)

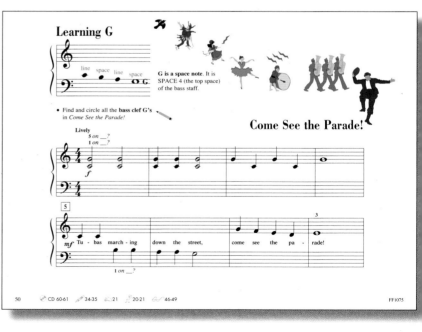

 The piano can imitate horns!

♪ ♫ Duet Appendix pp. 192-193    CD Tracks 60-61

partner pages

Theory
pp. 34-35 Bass Clef Parade

■ Students draw bass clefs, bass notes, and various rhythms. Sightreading and Ear-Training follow.

Technique & Artistry
p. 21 Catch Me If You Can!

■ A five-finger pattern moves up the keyboard. One hand prepares while the other hand plays!

Performance
pp. 20-21 Twinkle, Twinkle Little Star

■ Circle all the repeated notes.

■ Play LH with finger 4 or 3. Which do you prefer?

■ Double Cheese Sandwich!
 Help students memorize the form with this metaphor:
 Mm. 1-4 are a slice of fresh bread.
 Mm. 5-6 are a slice of cheese (or ham, turkey, etc.)
 Mm. 7-8 are another slice of cheese, etc.
 Mm. 9-12 is the bread on top.

■ (Play different sections for the student.)
 Is this the bread or the cheese? Remember your "sandwich" and play by memory.

Sightreading
pp. 46-49

pedagogy pointers

Here's a peppy way to introduce the G in the top space of the bass staff. The piece combines elements the student has played up to this point, and it is also the first 16-measure piece the student reads on the Grand Staff.

Playing by memory should be part of every lesson—whether a five-finger scale, two-measure pattern in a piece, or an entire tune. From the earliest lessons, create easy opportunities for the student to be successful with memory. Both Come See the Parade! and Twinkle, Twinkle Little Star offer elements of musical form for the student to hear—an introduction and ending, or "a double-cheese sandwich". Make memorizing memorable!

PIANO ADVENTURES VIDEO

see it in action

Teaching Video 45

Pointing to the notes at the top of the page, then finding them in the piece gets Vivian ready to play.

Then—what a merry medley! Vivian smartly marches through a collection of pieces. Come See the Parade! opens and closes the medley. Mister Bluebird, Driving in the G Clef, and A Ten-Second Song make up the middle. The snappy vamp keeps the tempo and meter steady and provides time to turn the pages and set up the next piece. Playing such a medley gives everyone a great sense of satisfaction and is a creative way to provide reinforcement.

Watch Vivian respond to the vamp as she gets ready for what's to come. Give this performance an E for enthusiasm!

Ask Yourself

■ How can you tell that Vivian feels the meter?

■ What are some of the advantages of having the student play a medley of pieces?

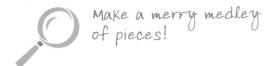

Make a merry medley of pieces!

S K I P S

Hey, Hey, Look at Me!

Lesson Book page 52

what's new

- Line-to-line skips on the staff
- Skips on the keyboard
- 1-3-5 finger combinations

what's important

- Reading line-to-line skips on the staff
- Skips with fingers 1-3-5

let's get started

1 Play skips from Middle C to the top. Use a braced third finger. I'll hold the pedal down. Magical sounds!

2 Super-duper challenge! Can you say the names of the keys as you skip from Middle C to the top? Go slowly.

3 When you skip notes, you also skip fingers. Let's test out some 1-3-5 skips (on the fallboard or table top).

4 Copy Cat. (Use 1-3-5 on C-E-G.) Repeat what I play. Can you make up skipping patterns for me to copy?

5 Hey, hey, let's play the piece!

explore & create

- **Hey, Hey, Play in F**
  Put your thumb on F and play again. Think line-to-line skips.

- **Hey, Hey, Play in G**
  Put your thumb on G and off you go!

- **Hey, Hey, Play Up the Keys**
  After you play it once, move your thumb to the very next key (D) and repeat the piece. Can you go all the way up the white keys to the next C? Hey, hey, let's play a duet!

  (See Video and Duet Appendix p. 194)

- **Skip It Your Way!**
  Put your RH fingers 1-3-5 over C-E-G. I'll play a duet. Listen to my beat and mood. You make up a melody using only C-E-G keys in any order. Nice skipping sounds!

  (See Video and Duet Appendix p. 195)

Reading thirds and playing thirds are separate skills.

108

 Duet Appendix pp. 194-195

 CD Tracks 62-63
4-measure IMPROVISATION at the end.
Students create their own melody using
Middle C-E-G skips.

partner pages

Theory
p. 36 Hey, Hey, Skip to the Ball!

- Line-to-line skips are presented first to foster success with this new reading concept.

- Students draw line-to-line skips to match the letter names and successfully land on the colored ball.

Performance
p. 22 Dancing with Frankenstein

- Frankenstein's line-to-line skips in the key of A minor pair nicely with the cheerful Hey, Hey, Look at Me! for this week's practice.

- After playing the song, let the student improvise on any white keys with the teacher duet. When you say, "Freaky Frankenstein", return and play the song once again.

Sightreading
pp. 50-53

pedagogy pointers

The student is introduced to skips on the staff and in the hand. At this point, skipping focuses only on recognizing and playing line-to-line thirds, and using only RH fingers 1-3-5. Begin by testing out alternating fingers on the fallboard or a flat surface. Call them "skipping fingers". That way, the student can concentrate on the coordination required without depressing keys or reading specific notes.

Referring to finger and note patterns continues the process of guiding the student to read and think in musical units.

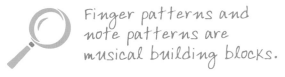 Finger patterns and note patterns are musical building blocks.

PIANO ADVENTURES VIDEO

see it in action

Teaching Video 46

Skipping is fun! And skipping in thirds up the keyboard makes a magical sound, especially if the pedal stays down while the thirds go higher and higher. Playing thirds requires finger coordination, so Vivian gets fingers 1-3-5 ready to go by testing out combinations on the fallboard and the keyboard. Then playing the piece is easy.

Music using thirds always sounds good, so why not make up your own piece that skips any way you'd like? The upbeat accompaniment sets a lively mood, and Vivian's fingers take off.

What if you began the piece starting on a new key? Ingrid goes on a real adventure, from C to C. Those skipping fingers get a real workout! Hey, Hey—she can play!

Ask Yourself

- What is evident when Vivian plays the thirds to the top of the keyboard?

- What does the teacher do when Vivian reads through the piece?

- What is noticeable about Ingrid's transposition sequence?

Allegro

Lesson Book page 53

S K I P S

what's new

- Playing hands together
- Allegro

what's important

- Playing hands together
- Reinforcing line-to-line skips
- Understanding what it means to play allegro

let's get started

1 Look at the RH in the first measure. Can you find the note and finger?

2 How many times does the pattern in measure one appear in the piece?

3 What's the difference between the RH in measures 1-2 and measures 5-6? Let's play these measures to hear the forte and piano.

4 Now add a LH C when you play that pattern. Let's play those measures once again.

5 In measures 3 and 4 the LH gets busy. Do the notes step or skip?

6 Compare Mm. 3-4 with Mm. 7-8. Do you see any changes?

explore & create

- **A Real Allegro Tempo**
  In Italian allegro means fast and lively. Let's play Allegro just that way. (Play the duet in the Lesson Book.)

- **Allegro Sailors**
  Go back to Hey, Hey, Look at Me! or Russian Sailor Dance and play these pieces allegro.

- **Meet the Composer**
  Mauro Giuliani taught himself how to play, and he was one of the most famous guitarists of his time. Beethoven was his friend and wrote some music for him. To see what Giuliani looked like, go to Google, type in his name, then click on "images". You'll also see how men dressed in those days.

partner pages

Theory
p. 37 Allegro Ride of Pegasus

■ For Eye-Training, students compose with skips to fill each empty measure with a whole note on C, E, or G. Fingers 1-3-5 play the Allegro Ride of Pegasus accompanied with a flowing teacher duet.

■ For Ear-Training, students play two half notes for each whole note written, creating a Half Note Variation.

Performance
p. 23 Donkeys Love Carrots

■ A traditional folk song using line-to-line skips pairs with the classical Allegro.

■ Extend the piece by playing the last two measures as a special ending up the piano! The teacher may accompany with the final measures of the duet.

pedagogy pointers

Allegro is packed with line-to-line thirds. Note that this time the right hand begins with the thumb on E. The hands played together in Best Friends, but this is the first time the right hand moves on its own, and the left hand is like an accompaniment.

The student learns that allegro means fast and lively, but also that it's important to first learn a piece slowly.

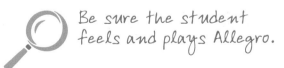 Be sure the student feels and plays Allegro.

PIANO ADVENTURES VIDEO

see it in action

Teaching Video 47

One secret to good reading is to be aware of what's the same and what's different. Ingrid is quick to make these comparisons, even to pointing out where it says "fast and lively" on the page. Learning the piece in sections reinforces this reading process. Because dynamic changes are included at the outset, musical playing is "built-in".

Holding the left-hand whole notes improves as the reading becomes secure. A cautious tempo is gradually upgraded. "Let's see what the Allegro speed feels like." Ingrid is ready to go, and the smooth, graceful duet is convincingly "fast and lively".

Ask Yourself

■ What is evident about the teacher's comments throughout the entire presentation?

■ How would you describe Ingrid's involvement?

S K I P S

Elephant Ride

Lesson Book page 54

what's new

- **Space-to-space skips on the staff**
- **4-2-2-4 finger combinations are used to play thirds**

what's important

- **Reading space-to-space thirds on the staff**
- **Playing thirds with fingers 2 and 4**

explore & create

- **Baby Elephant**
  Play the piece in a higher octave at a relatively quick tempo. (Make the duet sound sprightly.)

- **Mama Elephant**
  Play the piece in the middle of the keyboard at a tempo a bit slower than the Baby Elephant. (Make the duet sound rich.)

- **Daddy Elephant**
  Play the piece very low and slow.
  (Play the duet higher and fuller sounding.)

let's get started

1 (On the keyboard cover) Let's test how it feels to skip from (LH) 4-2 to (RH) 2-4. Those are the four legs of this elephant.

2 Notes can also skip from space to space. Look at measure 1. Those are the four legs! Try them out.

3 Can you see any other measures that are just like that one?

4 After those four legs skip up, they step down to E, for elephant.

5 In which measure do the notes step up and down from E?

6 Let's start the elephant slowly and keep him moving steadily.

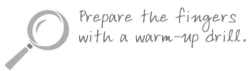

Prepare the fingers with a warm-up drill.

partner pages

Theory
p. 38 An Elephant Joke

■ Space-to-space and line-to-line skips are integrated with sightreading, note naming, and drawing skips.

Technique & Artistry
pp. 22-23 Skipping with Checkers

■ This sequential skipping pattern is quickly memorized so students may carefully watch their hand shape and feel the skips.

■ Repeat with fingers 2-4 to build finger coordination.

Performance
p. 24 I Like Roller Skating

■ Would you point out the skip(s) in each measure and tell me whether it is line-to-line or space-to-space?

■ If you looked at your feet rollerskating, you may run into something! Can you play this piece without ever looking at your hands?

Sightreading
pp. 54-57

pedagogy pointers

Now it's time to concentrate on space-to-space skips. In Elephant Ride, G-B-D-F is split between the hands to develop the student's experience with skips and to cover the wider distance (a seventh) from bottom to top. The 4-2 and 2-4 finger combinations are more challenging since the fourth finger is the least independent within the hand. Priming the finger skips as a warm-up drill prepares the hands to read the piece with greater ease.

Spinning off on the imagery from titles and lyrics will continue to be an invaluable teaching tool. Here, the idea of a family of elephants offers imaginative reinforcement of playing skips, feeling tempo, producing a variety of dynamics, and ensemble experience.

PIANO ADVENTURES VIDEO

see it in action

Teaching Video 48

This elephant needs four sturdy legs. Philip gets those fingers ready to move by trying out the 4-2-2-4 combination on the keyboard cover. From there, it's easy to see how those fingers fit the skips in the piece and become the elephant's four legs.

Those four legs get a good workout! After the skips, the elephant first swings his trunk down a bit, then he rests it by sitting quietly, and finally he swings it up and down to finish the ride.

A parakeet decides to accompany the heavy, stomping elephant. That elephant must weigh a ton! No wonder the parakeet twitters with excitement when the ride ends.

Ask Yourself

■ Which is easier—to move from the weak side of the hand (5-3-1 and 4-2) or the other way around (1-3-5 and 2-4)?

■ What does the teacher do when Philip tries out the piece?

UNIT 7

SKIPS

Yankee Doodle

Lesson Book page 55

what's new

- ■ **An introduction (of space-to-space skips)**

what's important

- ■ **Reinforcement of skips from space to space**
- ■ **Playing a familiar tune with good tone and spirit**

let's get started

1 I'll bet you know this song. Let's sing Yankee Doodle before we play it.

2 Now let's count and tap the rhythm in measures 1-4. Tap with the correct hand for each note.

3 The first four measures of this piece are an introduction to the song. Are the notes stepping or skipping?

4 Which notes do you play in these measures? Which fingers play? Get ready to play and count.

 Playing a well-known tune is satisfying.

explore & create

- ■ **Special Pedal Effect**
(Hold the pedal down while the student plays Mm. 1-4.) That makes the introduction sound really special. Would you like to hold the pedal? Perch on the edge of the bench and keep your heel on the floor.

- ■ **Your Own G-B-D-F "Doodle"**
Keep your fingers over the notes in Mm. 1-4. These are some "doodles" you might want to invent on your own. (Demonstrate a few patterns for the student to imitate.)

(See Video)

- ■ **Fancy-Schmancy Yankee Doodle**
Let's play a fancy duet version. After the introduction and the song, you improvise with G-B-D-F skips to my music. When I say, "Called it macaroni", return and play the song again. At the close, play Cs anywhere on the piano with a bang!

(See Video and Duet Appendix pp. 196-197)

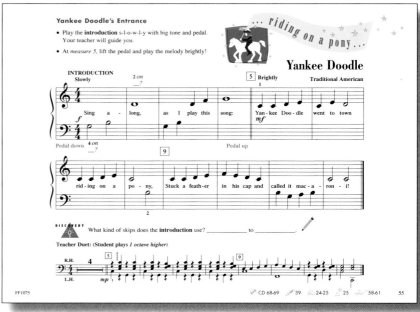

114

 Duet Appendix pp. 196-197   CD Tracks 68-69

partner pages

Theory
p. 39 Time for Playback!

- Ear-Training introduces students to "play back" a short C five-finger scale pattern that the teacher plays. (Teacher examples are provided.)

Technique & Artistry
pp. 24-25 Wheels Going 'Round

- Flowing space-to-space skips over the bar line is the crux of this little etude.

- Add dynamic changes and pedal for an artistic sound!

Performance
p. 25 The Happy Stream

- There are three skips in this piece. Can you find and circle them?

- There's one leap! Can you find and connect the notes with a wavy line like in the art?

- When well learned, try the piece at an allegro tempo.

Sightreading
pp. 58-61

pedagogy pointers

The introduction in Yankee Doodle announces with excitement what's coming next. Using the space notes that cut across the staff from bass to treble creates a "dominant" flourish that prepares the way for a familiar tune. With the pedal down, the introduction sounds especially "big time". This might be a chance for the student to hold down the pedal if the student can reach the floor comfortably, or if you have a pedal extension.

PIANO ADVENTURES VIDEO

see it in action

Teaching Video 49

Since the introduction is special, it's good to work out the rhythm before trying the notes. Once Vivian has learned the piece, she's ready for a challenge. By using different fingers on starting notes, she needs to read directionally. This also keeps her from equating Middle C as the "thumb" note.

The introduction notes then become a place where Vivian can "doodle" her own ideas. And this signals a rousing return to the song. Yankee Doodle rides off waving his feather in a flurry of Cs. Hats off, everyone!

Ask Yourself

- What counting system is used to prepare the introduction?

- How does the teacher prepare Vivian for her improvisation?

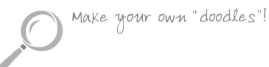
Make your own "doodles"!

Magic Rhyme for Bass D

Lesson Book page 56

what's new

- The name "Bass D key"
- Learning that LINE 3 in the bass clef is Bass D

what's important

- Knowing that Bass D is the first D BELOW Middle C and written on LINE 3 of the bass staff
- Knowing that any finger can play Bass D
- Dropping with arm weight for the forte notes; bouncing lightly and close to the key for the piano notes

3 Draw a WHOLE NOTE beside the one shown in the first measure. Let's do the same with the HALF NOTE in the next measure. Which way is the stem going?

4 This rhyme will help you remember Bass D: *Hey, diddle, diddle, D's in the middle.*

5 I'll demonstrate the piece. Watch me use my arm weight for the *forte* sound. Then I'll bounce lightly, close to the keys, for the soft ending. Sing the words to reinforce the location of Bass D.

6 Your turn! (Coach and compliment the student's technique.)

let's get started

1 Wave at the piano with your left hand. Now play the first D *below* Middle C. This is called Bass D. Play Bass D with LH finger 2, then 3, then 4.

2 Let's see what Bass D looks like on the bass staff. Study the staff at the top of the page. Is Bass D a LINE note or SPACE note? Which line is it written on? LINE 3 is the middle line, isn't it?

Discover the location of the key on the piano first, then teach its location on the staff.

explore & create

■ **Duet Magic**
Play the duet, singing the words.

■ **Find it Quick Game!**
Student closes eyes with hands in lap. The teacher calls out any left-hand finger. The student opens eyes and plays Bass D with that finger.

■ **Pencil Play**
Use blank staff paper. Student draws a bass clef. Teacher calls out one of these three bass LINE notes: Bass D, Bass F, or Bass A. The student draws a whole note on the correct line.

pedagogy pointers

Due to its visual placement on the MIDDLE LINE, Bass D is especially effective as a bass clef "Smart Note".

Stressing its location will prepare the student to easily read a step down (Bass C) and a step up (Bass E) in the next songs.

The rhyme, *"Hey, diddle, diddle, D's in the middle"*, offers an easy memory tool.

PIANO ADVENTURES VIDEO

see it in action

Teaching Video 50

Now it's time to extend reading in the Bass Clef. Middle D is a sure anchor. It's on the middle line, and it's in the middle of the two black keys. Easy!

Any finger can play this Smart Note. Charlotte tests them out, trying to balance on a rounded fingertip.

Writing Middle D on the staff confirms that Charlotte's eye focuses on the middle line, and she learns that the stem goes down. Drawing stems is a good way to translate information into action.

The words define the rhythm of the first two measures and Charlotte plays these firmly, bouncing softly as the piece tapers off. Soleil follows with a performance that includes the change to the second finger on the softer bounces.

Why not have fun with the new Ds. Copying rhythms opens the door to original experiments. And Charlotte rocks out a very peppy pattern!

Ask Yourself

■ What makes Charlotte happiest? What tells you that?

■ What is the value of encouraging students to play rhythms they cannot yet read?

A Joke for You

Lesson Book page 57

BASS C-D-E-F-G

what's new

- The name "Bass C key"

- Learning that Bass C is SPACE TWO, just below LINE 3 (Bass D)

- Learning that the stem on Bass C goes up and the stem on Bass D goes down.

what's important

- To quickly recognize Bass C as SPACE 2 with an upstem

- Knowing that any finger can play Bass C

let's get started

1 Play Bass D on the piano. Name the white key just below it. This is called Bass C. Play Bass C with LH finger 2, then 3, then 4. Note: Discover the location of the key on the piano first, then learn its location on the staff.

2 Let's see what Bass C looks like on the bass staff. Study the staff at the top of the page. Is Bass C a LINE note or SPACE note?

3 Which space is it written on? Notice that Bass C is a step below middle line D. Can you chant the memory rhyme for Bass D?

4 Notice the stem on Bass C goes up. (The teacher may explain stemming or wait until Level 1 where it is formally introduced.) Look at the next measure. The stem on Bass D goes down.

5 Now let's look at the piece. Measure 3 is an interesting measure. Point to the notes and say:
   C with an up-stem
   D with a down-stem
   C with an up-stem
   D with a down-stem
Note: Students often find reading this step confusing because of the stemming. Remind them to look at the noteheads.

6 Ask students to circle all the Bass Cs in the piece.

7 Play the piece once for the student, singing the words. Enjoy the play on words with "don-KEY" and "mon-KEY." Let the student play!

Learning Bass C
- Play Bass C—a step below Bass D.
- Look at the staff to the right.
  Bass C is on SPACE 2—just below middle line D.

The stem on Bass C goes up.* The stem on Bass D goes down.

A Joke for You
- Circle all the Bass C notes.

Cheerfully
f Can you name two keys that can't o-pen doors?

That would be a don-KEY and a mon-KEY, too!

*Teacher Note: The teacher may explain the rule that notes *below* the middle line have UP-stems. Stemming is taught in Level 1.

FF1075

CD 72-73   40   62-65   57

explore & create

- **Left Hand Finger Game**
  Can you play the piece again using LH fingers 2 and 1?

- **Find the Measure Game**
  I'm going to play measure 1, 2, 3, or 4. Close your eyes and listen. Then open your eyes and point to the measure I played.

partner pages

Theory
p. 40 Keychain Notes

- Students draw whole notes on Bass Clef D and Bass Clef C, then circle the keychains with a Bass Clef C.

- Drawing whole notes, quarter notes, and half notes on Bass Clef C reinforces its location and reviews rhythm values.

- Students review the 4/4 time signature by drawing one Bass Clef C (quarter, half, or whole note) to finish each incomplete measure.

Sightreading
pp. 62-65

pedagogy pointers

Students often find Bass C and Bass D confusing to read because of the stemming.

Take time for a closer look at the stemming, and remind students to focus on the noteheads.

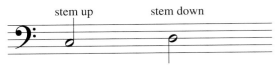

 Remind students that the stem on Bass Clef D goes down and the stem on Bass C goes up.

PIANO ADVENTURES VIDEO

see it in action

Teaching Video 51

Finding Bass C is simple if you use D-in-the-middle as the Smart Note guide. Soleil swoops down on Bass C, and Charlotte doesn't need reminding that Hey, diddle diddle is the quick reference.

Testing all those different fingers on the new note deflects the notion that the left hand always puts the fifth finger on Bass C.

Once again, writing the notes is a useful way to ensure that a student identifies an exact placement of new notes on the staff. But this is the first time that a note on the Bass Staff goes up. That's unusual! There are two ways to recognize the difference between the new bass notes—as line/space notes and by the direction of the stems. Both girls quickly report that in the piece the Cs and Ds rock back and forth.

The right hand answers the question posed by the left-hand Cs and Ds. Charlotte is soon zooming through the piece with confidence and energy.

Ask Yourself

- What does Charlotte play on Bass C even before she tests the finger changes?

- How does the teacher redirect Soleil's physical exuberance?

Football Game

Lesson Book page 58

what's new

- **Extension of the reading range in the bass clef**
- **Left-hand bass notes D and E**

what's important

- **Playing a left-hand C five-finger scale**
- **Playing with good tone and a steady tempo**

let's get started

1 You know Bass C and Bass F. Look at the example in the book. D and E fill in the space between. Which is the only note with a stem going up? (Bass C)

2 Shade in space 2 (Bass C) in the first measure of the second line of music. Can you name all the notes in that line?

3 Warming up means getting ready. Let's find some LH warm-up patterns and play each three times in a row (Mm. 1-2, 5-6, 7-8). (Improvise an accompaniment.)

4 The LH only steps and skips. What does the RH pattern do that's different? (Leap)

explore & create

- **Sports Announcer**
  Pretend that your hands are rival football teams. As you play the song, I'll be a sports announcer. Team A steps up the field. Team B leaps and steps down the field. (Continue for the rest of the piece.)

- **Field Goal**
  Can your LH kick a field goal at the end? Find the lowest C on the piano. Win the game!

  (See Video)

- **The Fans Are Dancing**
  Make the fans dance and celebrate using the LH C five-finger scale. (Play a vamp to set the tempo and mood.)

FF1075

partner pages

Theory
p. 41 Score a Touchdown!

■ Students notate the C five-finger scale with proper stemming in the bass clef, then use a winning note-reading strategy to name the footballs (with letter names) and score a touchdown!

Sightreading
pp. 66-69

pedagogy pointers

The new octave-apart hand placement is called the C five-finger scale. Moving the left hand to begin on a Bass C extends the reading range in the bass clef. The space between Bass C and Bass F and G is now filled in. The piece gives the left hand a chance to play the notes in the five-finger scale up and down, stepping and skipping.

 "Hey, diddle, diddle, D's in the middle" is a memorable hook that helps in learning the Bass E (a step above) and the Bass C (a step below).

PIANO ADVENTURES VIDEO

see it in action

Teaching Video 52

First there's a warm-up to the warm-up! Philip practices the left-hand trick (skipping up and down from the new Bass C), then the right-hand trick (playing the broken fifth). That reinforces the skipping finger-feel and prepares him for those measures in which there is a change from notes that step up or down.

A low C is added as the "field goal". Philip quickly connects these activities to his own world. The high kick is the big event. The referee signals touchdown!

Ask Yourself

■ On which finger does the "field goal" land?

■ Which "tricks" could you invent for a girl, or someone other than a football fan?

 Warm-up "tricks" get the hands ready.

B A S S · C - D - E - F - G

Octavius the Octopus

Lesson Book page 59

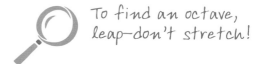

what's new

■ **Octave**

what's important

■ **Finding octaves up and down**

■ **Playing LH octaves by leaping, not stretching**

■ **Recognizing Bass C**

let's get started

1 How many legs does that octopus have? If you count down 8 keys from this C, where do you land?

2 Eight keys up or down from any key is called an octave. The keys will have the same name—C to C or G to G.

3 Play an octave HIGHER from the C I play. Now the E. The F. Now play an octave LOWER from the D I play. Now the G. The A.

4 You can play an octave with one hand. Put your LH thumb on C, then leap down an octave. Jump back and forth.

5 How many times does this piece jump down an octave? (4) Can you describe how to find Bass C on the staff? Where is that Bass C on the staff? (Hint: Space two, or a step below middle line D.)

6 Let's name the notes aloud from M. 5 to the end. Are you stepping or skipping?

7 Tap the rhythm while I play and sing the piece. Demonstrate, then let the student play Octavius the Octopus.

To find an octave, leap—don't stretch!

explore & create

■ **Octave Bells**

Create octave bell sounds. Let the student depress the damper pedal and play octave Cs across the piano. Use finger 3 braced with the thumb.

■ **Step and Skip and Octave Hunt**

Ask the student to follow your directions starting from Bass C. For example:

Play Bass C
Play UP an octave (Middle C)
Play up a skip (E)
Play DOWN an octave (E)
Play up a step (F)
Play UP an octave (F)
Play down a skip (D)
Play down a step (C)
Where did you land? (Middle C)

Make up more on your own!

pedagogy pointers

Octopus to octaves—eight arms, eight keys—is a natural connection to a new concept. Finding octaves higher and lower then becomes an easy trick. At this stage, it's important not to stretch the hand too far, so the left hand leaps from top to bottom.

This is also a chance to introduce Bass C as the note an octave lower than Middle C. Although the piece is short, you can use it as a launching pad for other octave-related games and ideas.

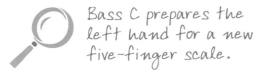

Bass C prepares the left hand for a new five-finger scale.

PIANO ADVENTURES VIDEO

see it in action

Teaching Video 53

Octave is a new idea. Philip counts out the distance between notes with the same name. Finding octaves up and down is proof that he understands the concept.

Playing octaves with one hand is also a new skill. This is the first time that a hand changes position within a piece. Philip, Soleil, and Charlotte each practice hopping back and forth. That's a big jump for a smaller hand. Aim that finger!

Playing on the closed lid gives Soleil a chance to prepare both the rhythm of the piece and the left-hand moves. Added to stepping and skipping is leaping.

On her first try, Soleil's third finger almost runs up the scale from C to C. The giant octopus plays along to keep the baby octopus from swimming away. Charlotte's solo Octopus knows exactly how to leap and how to step up that scale. Steady as she goes!

Ask Yourself

■ How does the teacher "correct" Philip's errors and hesitations when finding octaves?

■ Besides doubling Soleil's part an octave lower, how does the teacher keep the baby Octopus steady?

Copy Cat

Lesson Book page 60

what's new

- **To imitate notes and rhythms between the hands**
- **Playing "harmonic skips" with these finger combinations: 1-3, 2-4, 3-5**

what's important

- **Hearing, seeing, and understanding imitation**
- **Using dynamic contrasts for different motives**
- **Exploring different finger combinations for skips**

let's get started

1 Are you a good copy cat? Copy what I do (stand, sit, bow, wink). Copy my rhythm. (Tap a rhythm.) Copy my hand position. (C five-finger scale.)

2 See if you can copy my music message. (Use patterns from the piece: Mm. 1 and 2, Mm. 5 and 6, and so on. You are preparing the student's fingers for the steps and skips in the piece.)

3 Look over this piece. Which hand is the Copy Cat?

4 Which parts are *forte?* Which are *piano?*

explore & create

- **Copy What I Play**
  Find the C five-finger scale, either hand. Watch, then copy what I play. (Create short melodies one octave lower for the student to play back.) Then change hands and continue the game.

- **Copy Cat with Eyes Closed**
  Could you be a copy cat with your eyes closed? (Continue playback patterns.)

- **You Can Be the Leader!**
  Make up a pattern in the C five-finger scale for me to copy. Choose whichever hand you like.

- **You Copy What You Play**
  Let your RH make up a pattern for your LH to copy. Try several more. Now switch. Is each hand a good copy cat? (See Video)

partner pages

Theory
p. 42 Copycat Meows!

■ Students identify two-note "cat meows" as a step or skip in the bass clef.

■ Next, students copy each example neatly, name the notes in the balls of yarn, and play each step or skip on the piano.

Technique & Artistry
p. 26 Pilot in the Clouds

■ This sequenced skipping pattern spans the inside to the outside of the hand and back: 1-3-5-3-1.

■ Students should play by memory to observe their hand shape.

■ Aim to play at a brisk, allegro tempo.

Performance
p. 26 Are You Sleeping?

■ Do you see any copy catting in this piece? Tell me about this.

■ Circle the four skips.

■ When well learned, try playing as a round (second part begins at M. 3).

Sightreading
pp. 70-73

pedagogy pointers

The student has "copied" before, as in I Hear the Echo, but there it was for the purpose of introducing forte and piano. Here the focus is on imitation of rhythmic and melodic patterns. This develops the student's awareness of how imitation is used as a compositional element.

It's important for the student to see that a pattern is imitated elsewhere—this supports fluent reading—but also very important to make sure that a student hears imitation since imitation almost always invites dynamic change.

PIANO ADVENTURES VIDEO

see it in action

Teaching Video 54

Imitating someone is fun, and Tatiana doesn't miss a trick! By copying keyboard "messages", she's prepared for those places in the piece at which there might be a stumble or hesitation. Playing Copy Cat then becomes easy, and she can pay attention to dynamics from the start.

Singing while playing encourages a sense of phrasing. Reacting to the accompaniment, she ends the duet with a natural ritard. Tatiana's original copy cats are certainly frisky and adventurous!

Ask Yourself

■ Why is it especially impressive that Tatiana copies the left hand so well?

■ What can you glean about Tatiana from her original copy cat messages?

 See what's the same. Hear what's the same.

Grandmother

Lesson Book pages 62-63

what's new

- Musical question
- Parallel and contrasting musical answer

what's important

- To recognize parallel and contrasting musical answers
- To begin creating parallel and contrasting answers

let's get started

1 Listen! Mm. 1-4 ask a musical question. (Play and sing. Playfully plead, "Gra-and-mother" to stress the opening note.)

2 Let's examine Mm. 3-4. Where do you skip? Where do you step? Your turn to try the musical question!

3 The piece continues with a musical answer. Notice the answer ends on the home note, C. It sounds like the end. (Have the student play the musical answer.)

4 The LH has some added notes to make the melody sound fancier. Let's play just the last "cher-ry pie" measure hands together. (Try several times.)

5 Ready to play the last four measures with both hands? (Sing the words as the student plays.)

6 Let's hear the entire piece. (The teacher may sing verse 2 to emphasize the question and answer.)

explore & create

- **Musical Question and Answer**
  A musical question may end on any note except the "home note". Does the question in Grandmother end on the home note? (No) The music sounds incomplete, as if it needs an answer.
  A parallel answer begins the SAME as the question. Then it changes and ends on the "home note". It sounds complete. Does the answer in Grandmother begin the same as the question? (Yes) It is a parallel answer. Let's try it out!
  A contrasting answer begins DIFFERENTLY from the question and ends on the "home note". Here's the same question with a contrasting answer. Try it out!

- **A Musical Conversation**
  (Use the C five-finger scale.) Teacher plays this musical question:
  Ex. 1 2 3 4 5 — 5 — 1 2 3 4 5 — — —
  Student plays a PARALLEL answer.
  Repeat the same question. Student plays a CONTRASTING answer.

- **More Conversations**
  (Choose parallel, contrasting, or both)
  Ex. 1 3 5 — 1 3 5 — 5 4 3 2 3 — — —
  Ex. 1 2 3 4 3 2 1 — 2 3 4 5 4 3 2 —
  Ex. 5 — 3 — 5 — 3 — 5 5 3 3 5 — — —

partner pages

Technique & Artistry
p. 27 Canoeing Upstream

■ The two-measure canoe stroke must pass evenly from left to right hand. No splashes!

■ Play slowly with pedal for a peaceful sound.

■ Play with both hands starting on F or G.

Theory
p. 43 Questions and Answers

■ For Eye-Training, students sightread and identify each question and answer.

■ For Ear-Training, students listen and identify each parallel or contrasting answer.

Performance
p. 27 Horseback Riding

■ Galloping skips in 3/4 encourage feeling this ride with one beat per measure.

■ Begin on G or A (all white keys)!

Sightreading
pp. 74-77

pedagogy pointers

In Grandmother, the left hand leads with a melody that uses all the notes in the C five-finger scale. It also provides an accompaniment for the answering right-hand melody, and it's in position to sing a duet with the right hand in the last measure. The coordination between the hands is the most required so far, but the fact that it lies so well within the hand makes it relatively easy.

The words as well as the musical motives invite experimentation with question and answer phrasing. This can be between teacher and student, between student and student, and by a single student "answering" an original question with the opposite hand.

PIANO ADVENTURES VIDEO

see it in action

Teaching Video 55

A performance with accidental changing meters is "evened out" by an expressive explanation rather than a correction. Tatiana responds quickly and moves into the repeat with a natural sense for completing the second verse.

Transposing the piece to G is simple, and once again Tatiana wants to get to that chocolate cake!

Since the words for each of the first phrases are questions, this is a perfect place to create original questions and answers. It's clear that her musical instincts are guiding Tatiana's answers back to the home tone. This is ear training in action!

Ask Yourself

■ Why does Tatiana first say that she's playing in the G scale?

■ How does the teacher respond when Tatiana continues singing?

■ How does the teacher introduce the question and answer process?

THE TIE

Lemonade Stand

Lesson Book pages 64-65

what's new

- **The Tie**
- **Playing ties in a simple setting**

what's important

- **The Tie: what it means and what it looks like**
- **Counting and playing a steady 3/4 beat**

let's get started

1 If you wanted to make a piece of rope longer, what could you do? (Tie another piece of rope to it.) We can do the same thing in music—connect notes together with a curved line called a tie.

2 Listen and look while I play Lemonade Stand. See if you can spot the ties. At the tie, did I play or hold the dotted half note twice?

3 Let's tap the piece on the keyboard cover, counting 1-2-3. At the tie we'll count 1-2-3, tie-2-3. Use both hands.

4 Let's tap the piece again, using the hands as in the piece. Count, or sing the words. (1-2-3, tie-2-3).

explore & create

- **Let's Tie It Up!**
  (Draw examples of notes tied together.) How many total beats will the key be held? Now you draw some tied notes for me. Did I get the answer right?

- **A New Location!**
  Move your Lemonade Stand to the G Street.

- **New Flavors!**
  Can you think of something else to sell that fits the "lem-on-ade" rhythm? (For example, "straw-ber-ries," "blue-ber-ries," "choc-o-late," etc.)

 Words often convey a rhythm or meter better than counting.

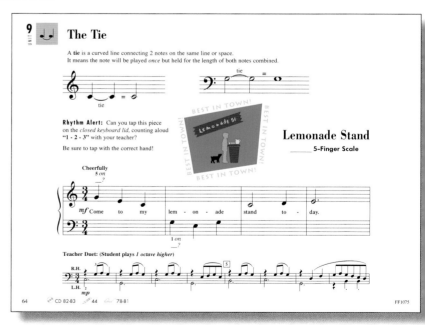

partner pages

Theory
p. 44 Let's Buy Lemonade

■ Students connect the two notes in each "glass of lemonade" with a tie, then add up the beats to see how many pennies they will owe.

Sightreading
pp. 78-81

pedagogy pointers

This piece introduces the tie. The tie goes over the measure bar, connecting notes at the ends of phrases. Since the piece is in 3/4 meter, the ties connect dotted half notes. The tie at the half cadence is preceded by two measures of quarter notes, setting up the impetus for feeling three beats to the bar.

Switching from one hand to the other happens quite quickly. Because these switches involve many skips, the eye must scan the directional note movement rapidly. The final performance of the piece should move with a lilting swing.

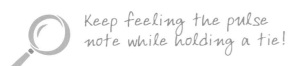
Keep feeling the pulse note while holding a tie!

PIANO ADVENTURES VIDEO

see it in action

Teaching Video 56

Holding long notes for their full value after a succession of quicker notes may be a challenge. David's natural energy results in good tone and continuity even when he transposes, although a few of the longer notes are rushed.

A rhythm "accident" can also easily be repaired. Words often capture a rhythm or meter with more natural ease than counting. The tap-clap-clap routine helps Alexis feel and respond in 3/4 meter. It's clear, however, that when Alexis finishes the piece as part of a duet, she has internalized the rhythms and meter and understands "tie". It's the "best lemonade in town".

Ask Yourself

■ Why do you think that David finds it easier to play pieces in G?

■ Why do you think Alexis makes that particular rhythmic error?

■ What do you notice about Alexis's eye movement in the final performance?

All My Friends

Lesson Book page 66

THE TIE

what's new

- ■ **Ties from weak beats to downbeats**
- ■ **Syncopation**

what's important

- ■ **Feeling the tie**
- ■ **Feeling the syncopation**

let's get started

1 Copy what I tap. (Tap the rhythm of Mm. 1-2 with strong syncopation). Tap it with your RH. Your LH. Now hands together.

2 Let's play that rhythm pattern on C (or any key).

3 This is what that rhythm looks like in the music. (Point to Mm. 1-2, then point to the tie.) What's this? The tie goes over the bar line.

4 You point to the notes while I play the piece. Point with whichever hand plays the part.

5 Let's work at the piece in two-measure sections. Play Mm. 1-2 five times for the five letters in Jimmy. Then play

Mm. 3-4 three times for Ben; Mm. 5-6 four times for Sara. (Sing the words.)

6 Now let's gather all your friends together. Play the piece.

explore & create

- ■ **New Rhythm Cheers**
  Have fun chanting these syllables to the rhythm pattern in Mm. 1-2:

  bah bah bah BOOM   bah bah
  va va va VOOM   va va

  Make up your own silly words!

- ■ **Play Rhythm Cheers**
  Play your rhythm cheer on any key, a drum, a triangle, or with maracas.

- ■ **Ear Patterns**
  RH fingers over the C five-finger scale. Close your eyes! I'll play that rhythm pattern using any of these notes. See if you can copy me. Let's try this with your LH!

partner pages

Theory
p. 45 Tricky Measures / All Ears!

■ For Eye-Training, students must count the beats and spot incorrect "lemon" measures, then draw a big X through each!

■ For Ear-Training, students "play back" rhythms with ties that the teacher plays using the C five-finger scale.

Technique & Artistry
p. 28 We Won the Game Today!

■ A syncopated pattern travels up and down the keys. Let's clap and say the words before playing.

■ Can you play each hand with your eyes closed? Feel the keys!

Sightreading
pp. 82-85

pedagogy pointers

Everyone likes to play music with a little "zip" in it. Ties are often used to create syncopated effects. In this second piece that uses ties, the ties are from weak beats to downbeats, not on ending notes where holding notes over the bar line is often expected. Here again, it's important that the student first *feel* the syncopation, then see that it is caused by the tie.

Each time, the skip is to the tied note, and the rhythm pattern that includes the tie is used three times in succession. It becomes a rhythmic motive that reinforces how the tie creates the syncopated effect.

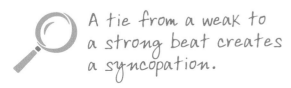
A tie from a weak to a strong beat creates a syncopation.

PIANO ADVENTURES VIDEO

see it in action

Teaching Video 57

Emily first copies the rhythm pattern before she learns what it looks like in note values. Pointing to the notes helps her see how the tie creates the syncopated feeling. Working in two-measure sections reinforces the rhythm and prepares her for reading the piece fluently.

The constant quarter notes in the duet part also help to highlight the syncopation. Using the pattern in an ear-training game completes the syncopated cycle. What zippy friends!

Ask Yourself

■ What's especially effective when Emily points to the notes as the teacher plays?

■ How does the teacher organize the ear-training melodic patterns?

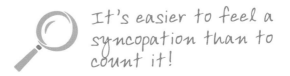
It's easier to feel a syncopation than to count it!

Bells of Great Britain

Lesson Book page 67

THE TIE

what's new

- **Playing a tie with added notes in the opposite hand**
- **Exploring pedal and dynamics across the keyboard range**
- **Double tie**

what's important

- **Good forte and piano contrasts**
- **Moving the RH gracefully**

let's get started

1 Listen to the bells! (Play the piece for the student.)

2 Let's pretend we're ringing bells! Use big gestures for loud bells, small gestures for soft bells, and big, slow circles for the dotted half notes. (Demonstrate)

(See Video)

3 When the bells move higher, do they get louder or softer? Prepare the RH moves (gentle lifts) in Mm. 9-11.

4 Listen to these bells again while I use the pedal. (Mm. 9-12) How would you describe the sound?

5 Bells from many churches often ring at the same time. Keep the pedal down through the whole piece and hear all the bells ring. Hold and listen at the end.

explore & create

- **To Ring or Not to Ring**
  (Have the student play the piece with the pedal, then without.) How would you describe the difference?

- **Listen Up**
  Close your eyes. I'm going to play some music, sometimes with pedal, sometimes not. Tell me: Is it with pedal, or without pedal?

- **Bells in G and F**
  Let's visit some other bell towers. Play the piece with fingers over the G scale, or over the F scale.

- **If You Have a Grand Piano**
  Let's look inside and see what the pedal does. (Demonstrate and explain.) Now you know what dampers look like and what happens when you hold the pedal down.

The piano's special effects can be thrilling!

partner pages

Technique & Artistry
p. 29 Peaceful Sunset

■ Discuss heavy arms (arm weight) for the opening RH notes, and a light touch for the LH.

■ For Mm. 3-4, try playing the RH Es up in octaves as the color spreads across the sky.

■ Try playing in F and G positions.

Performance
p. 28-29 Trumpet Song

■ This baroque theme presents the RH melody against LH sustained notes.

■ More complex interplay of steps and skips presents a reading and technical challenge using notes of the C five-finger scale.

pedagogy pointers

There are several new elements that make Bells of Great Britain special. Not only does the right hand play harmonic thirds, but the last third is connected by a double tie while the left hand plays softly on the "tied" notes.

Students love to use the pedal, and holding the damper pedal down throughout this piece creates the ringing sonorities associated with bells. When the right-hand thirds move higher in each measure and begin to fade in the distance, the richness of the sound is truly pianistic. You might even try that left-hand fifth an octave lower!

Presenting this piece using big rhythmic motions (as in the video) is an ideal way to help ensure that the student experiences the relative lengths of different note values and the change of energy used to make louder and softer sounds.

 Big rhythmic gestures help the student internalize the rhythm.

PIANO ADVENTURES VIDEO

see it in action

Teaching Video 58

Patrick really rings those bells! The loud bells need big motions, the dotted half notes swing a full circle, and the soft bells are played with restraint. Not only does this prepare the sound of the piece, but it also translates the musical concepts into full body motions, the best way to help Patrick internalize the melody, rhythm, and dynamics. His own keyboard performance demonstrates that he has internalized these concepts.

There are graceful "rainbows" when Patrick moves to the higher octaves, and he listens carefully as the last tones die away. Beautiful bells!

Ask Yourself

■ How does the teacher present the bell-ringing?

■ What's special about the way Patrick ends his performance?

Come On, Tigers!

Lesson Book page 68

what's new

- Quarter rest

what's important

- To hear a quarter rest
- To recognize a quarter rest
- To respond to a quarter rest

let's get started

1 Sometimes in music we have moments of silence—rests.

2 I'll play some music. Each time you hear a rest, raise your hand.

(See Video and Duet Appendix p. 198)

3 This fancy little squiggle (point to it) is the sign for a quarter rest. Whenever you see one, take a rest!

4 Let's do the Go Team chant (see the page). Tap for each word, and make a loose fist for each rest.

5 Ready over the C five-finger scale. Let's cheer for Our Team!

explore & create

- **Go Team Chant on C-G**
  Hands over the C five-finger scale.
  Play C and G together, both hands. Now let's play the Go Team chant.

  (Duet Appendix p. 199)

- **Go Team Chant on G-D**
  Let's chant for the G team. Fingers over G and D. Hooray!

- **Our Team Is Down Low**
  Your team has a 300-lb. star player. Find the lowest C five-finger scales and play Come On, Tigers! to cheer him on. (Play a forceful accompaniment.)

  (Duet Appendix p. 199)

"Resting" must be an active—not a passive—experience.

 Duet Appendix pp. 198-199

 CD Tracks 88-89
8-measure IMPROVISATION at the end.
Students explore using quarter rests with
their own C five-finger scale melody.

partner pages

Theory
pp. 46-47 Tiger Cheer

■ Students trace and draw quarter rests.

■ Student and teacher tap the Tiger Cheer in various ways, observing all the quarter rests!

Technique & Artistry
p. 30 Our Team Scores Again!

■ A quarter rest on beat 1 helps each hand prepare the fifth.

■ Contrary motion makes playing skips with hands together accessible and fun!

■ The half note at the end of every two measures helps the "team members" wind down and concentrate on firm fingertips.

pedagogy pointers

Hearing what it means to rest is the most important element in teaching the quarter rest. Watching for, and responding to, rests in the peppy chant is the next step. Substituting a gesture for each rest makes observing rests an active, rather than a passive, experience.

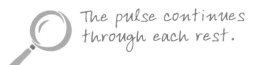 *The pulse continues through each rest.*

PIANO ADVENTURES VIDEO

see it in action

Teaching Video 59

Vivian has fun responding to the challenge of the chant. She begins to expect the rests to follow a pattern, but catches the change. That's careful listening!

When she plays the chant on the piano, it's clear from her body language that Vivian is feeling the rests. Absolutely thumbs up!

Playing Come On, Tigers! is easy and especially full of energy and zip when a performance low on the keyboard is for the big guy on the team. Win! Win!

Ask Yourself

■ Can you think of another activity for the student to demonstrate hearing a rest?

■ Why is the chant effective in teaching what it means to "rest"?

■ What's different about the second (duet) performance?

Princess or Monster?

Lesson Book page 69

what's new

- **Quarter rest in a more challenging context**
- **Steps and skips using C five-finger scale notes**

what's important

- **Releasing the keys on all the quarter rests**
- **Finger coordination on all the skips**

let's get started

1 Look at the title of this piece—Princess or Monster? You choose! First, I'll play the piece singing the words for the princess (or monster). Will you point to the notes and rests while I play?

2 (Put the lid down.) Now let's tap and chant the words. The princess/monster is slowly walking through the castle/dungeon. (For the rests, make a quick, loose fist. Or, open hands, palms up.) Repeat at a faster tempo. The princess/monster is running!

3 Let's circle all the skips in the music. Is there a skip in M. 1? M. 2? (Continue in this way.)

4 Put your RH in the C five-finger scale. We can use three different finger groups to play skips. First, play back and forth with fingers 1 and 3.

5 Another combination is 2 and 4. Let's play back and forth with fingers 2 and 4. Can you guess the third one? (Fingers 3-5)

6 What skipping fingers do you play in measure 2? (Fingers 1-3) Measure 3? (Fingers 2-4) Measure 4? (Fingers 3-5)

7 Play and keep "tuned in" so you hear silence on each rest. Ready for the royal duet? The monster duet?

explore & create

- **The Princess/Monster Is Tired**
  Play her music slowly and sweetly. Play his loudly, stomping around!

- **The Princess/Monster Runs**
  Play his/her music quickly, but don't forget the rests!

  Optional: Have the princess/monster play in G (Duet Appendix p. 200)

- **Your Own Skipping Melody**
  Let's experiment with your own C scale melody that uses skips with fingers 1-3, 2-4, and 3-5. I'll play a duet. You create a melody that skips.

  (See Video and Duet Appendix p. 201)

partner pages

Technique & Artistry
p. 31 What the Queen Told the King

- For this finger exercise, different skipping combinations (fingers 1-3, 2-4, 3-5) are punctuated by quarter rests.

- The quarter rests gives one beat to prepare the next finger grouping.

- Keep the conversation between the Queen and King slow until each finger knows the way!

Performance
pp. 30-31 Rain, Rain, Go Away

- Fingers 1 and 3 skip together in parallel motion to begin three out of the four phrases.

- At measure 9, use the rest to lift your hand to the next higher C.

Sightreading
pp. 86-89

pedagogy pointers

The quarter rest was introduced on the preceding page, and here the quarter rest highlights the moments of silence after "princess/monster" and "castle/dungeon". Make sure the key is released, not held as a half note. The student must be alert. "Princess" and "castle" are punctuated by rests, but in one spot the rhythm to these words changes to half notes.

The melody has many skips. Checking and drilling these in advance will prepare the student for the coordination required to read and play the piece smoothly.

PIANO ADVENTURES VIDEO

see it in action

Teaching Video 60

Using the hands as they appear in the piece, Emily taps and "rests" while the princess first glides, then runs through the castle.

Why not let the princess test her finger-skipping skills by creating her own melodies?

How easily a princess can become a monster living in a dungeon! A stomping, monster-like accompaniment encourages David to play boldly. His hesitation to repeat is quickly overcome by inviting the monster to play in another key!

Ask Yourself

- Many students will have the same hesitations as Emily does when she taps the piece at different tempos. What happens?

- Does David's monster always rest when he should?

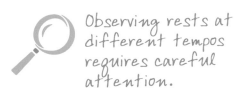

Observing rests at different tempos requires careful attention.

The Bugle Boys

Lesson Book pages 70-71

what's new
- **The end of the book**

what's important
- **A peppy tempo**
- **Strong dynamic contrasts**
- **Clear rests**
- **Getting the left hand ready for the changing positions**

let's get started

1 At the end this band marches away. The farther it goes, the softer it gets.

2 Each time it repeats, the left hand moves one octave lower. Let's try those moves down the keyboard.

3 When the band is close (the first time), it's forte. When it moves, it's mezzo forte— then (down low) piano.

4 Let's make sure we hear the right-hand and left-hand rests. Hup (rest) Hup (rest) Hup 2-3-4.

5 Ready to march!

explore & create

- **Piccolo Start-Up**
  The piccolos tune up to start off the parade. Listen, get ready—march!

  (See Video)

- **The F Company Band**
  Another band joins the parade. (Student transposes to F.)

- **The G Company Band**
  Here comes another band! (Start in the G five-finger scale.)

- **March with Us**
  Is there a drummer or triangle player in the house who would like to march along with these bands?

- **The Entertaining Bugle Boys**
  "The Entertainer" joins the Bugle Boys for a spectacular finish.

  (See Video and Duet Appendix pp. 202-203)

It's the end!

 *Congratulations!*

 Duet Appendix pp. 202-203    CD Tracks 94-95

partner pages

Theory
pp. 48 The Bugle Boys Quiz

- A final Bugle Boys Quiz reviews notes, musical concepts, and rhythms to complete the book.

Technique & Artistry
p. 32 Leading the Parade

- Some technical mistakes stem from poor rhythm and vice versa.

- This little etude presents all note values from the Primer in strict march time.

- A perfect steady beat will help fingers march on the tips. Remember to sit tall, too!

Performance
p. 32 Let's Boogie!

- Point out four measures that skip up.

- Point out two measures that repeat.

- Point out a measure that steps up. A measure that steps down.

- Let's clap it first. We'll make a loose fist during the rest.

- Ready to play!

Sightreading
pp. 90-95

pedagogy pointers

It's a good idea to set up the introduction and ending first. They are similar, but different. The moves and dynamic changes at the end are made easier by advance preparation.

This is the "graduation" piece. It represents what has been achieved at the end of the Primer Book. And what a spirited finale it is!

PIANO ADVENTURES VIDEO

see it in action

Teaching Video 61

Philip follows the teacher's model, then marches on his own. It's important to remember that as the left hand descends, the dynamics need to reflect the departing buglers.

The piccolos announce the start of the parade, and they're off! This energetic band moves at a perky tempo and plays with solid tone. Philip's eyes really track ahead to ensure those left-hand moves. The drums fade away gradually as the parade disappears down the street. Then—the all-star "entertaining" parade. What a send-off. Salute!

Ask Yourself

- To compliment Philip on his first duet performance, what would you single out?

- What is noticeable about the performance when the "Entertainer" parades with the "Bugle Boys"?

 *Hats off to these Bugle Boys!*

Finger Flashcard Music

Lesson Book p. 7:
Finger Flashcards   Video 4

Student plays Flashcards in rhythm on the key cover.

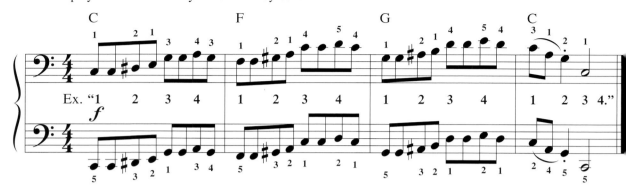

Two Blackbirds
Turn into Two Snowflakes

Lesson Book p. 11:
Two Blackbirds   Video 7

Student plays Two Blackbirds using the two white keys C-D.

Snow Swirls at the Piano

Lesson Book p. 11:
Two Blackbirds   Video 7

Student improvises using any high white keys.

DUET APPENDIX

Six Little Kittens

Lesson Book p. 13:
Three Little Kittens   Video 9

Student plays Three Little Kittens.

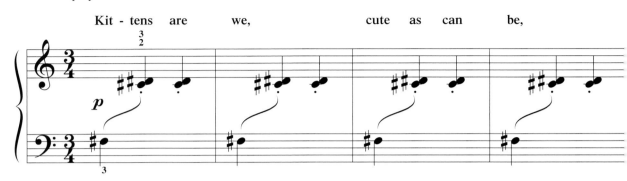

Kit - tens   are   we,   cute   as   can   be,

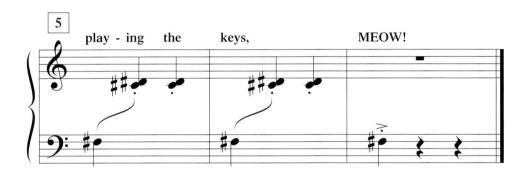

play - ing   the   keys,   MEOW!

DUET APPENDIX

The Quarter Note Song

Lesson Book p. 14:
The Quarter Note   Video 10

Student and teacher sing.

It's got a | head and a stem, and it's | all col-ored in._____ It's got a

head and a stem, and it's | all col-ored in._____ It's got a

head and a stem, and it's | all col-ored in._____

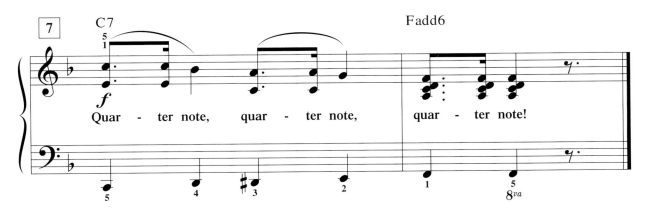

Quar - ter note, quar - ter note, | quar - ter note!

143

Quarter Notes with Haydn!

from Franz Joseph Haydn's Concerto in C for piano

Lesson Book p. 14:
The Quarter Note   Video 10

Teacher and student set a steady beat on Gs. Student continues playing Gs as teacher plays the rest of the piece.

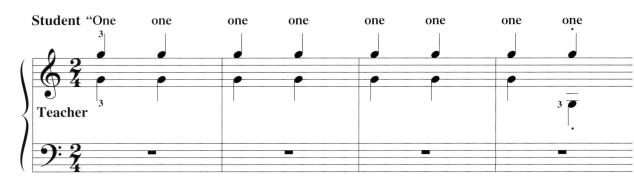

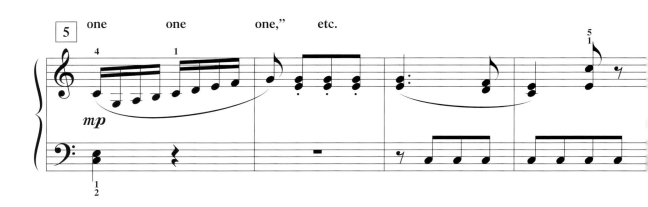

D U E T   A P P E N D I X

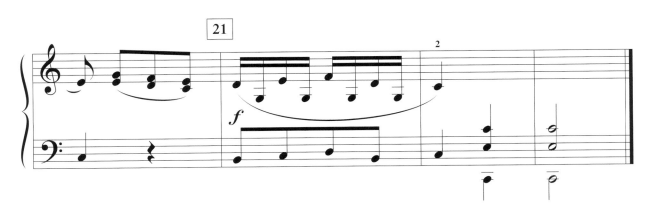

Old Clock Gongs

Lesson Book p. 15:
The Old Clock   Video 11

Student improvises long and short "chime and gong sounds" on higher two-black-key groups.

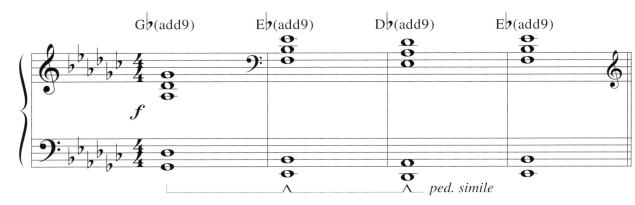

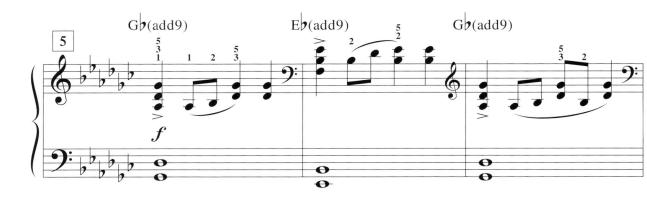

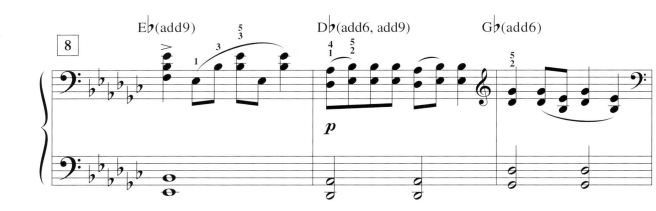

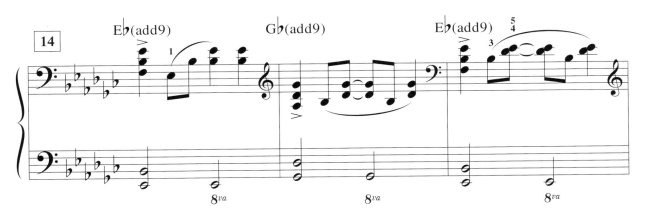

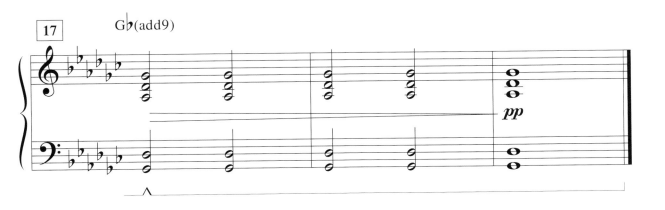

All Kinds of Walking!

Lesson Book p. 16:
The Walking Song   Video 12

Quarter-note accompaniment for The Walking Song. Student plays 1 octave higher.

The King's Walk

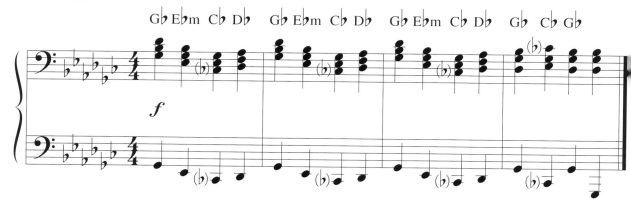

Eighth-note accompaniment for The Walking Song. Student plays 1 octave higher.

Clown Walk

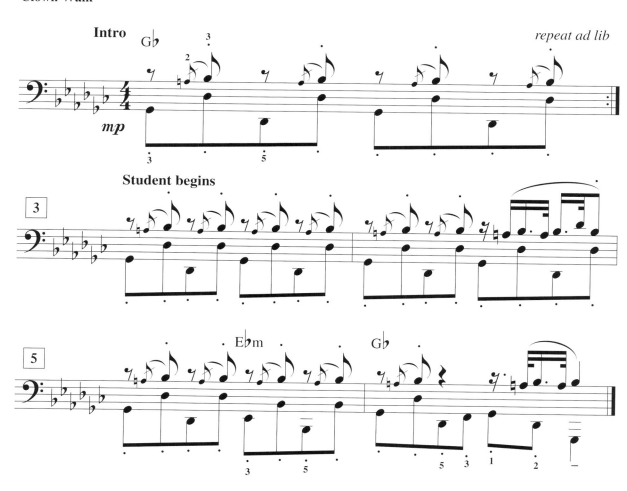

Triplet accompaniment for The Walking Song. Student plays 1 octave lower.

The Swing

Sixteenth-note accompaniment for The Walking Song. Student plays as written.

The Tooth Fairy

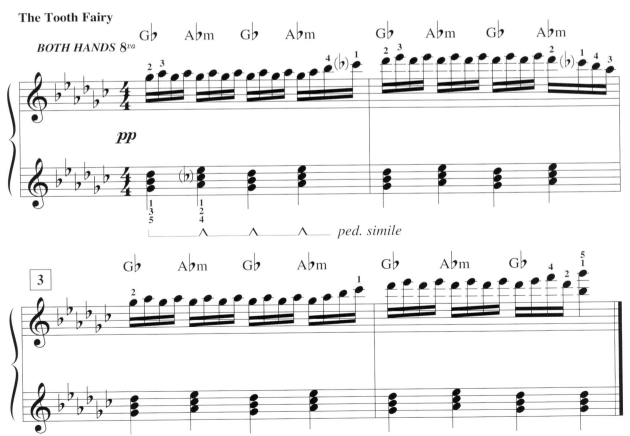

The Half Note Song

Teacher and student sing.

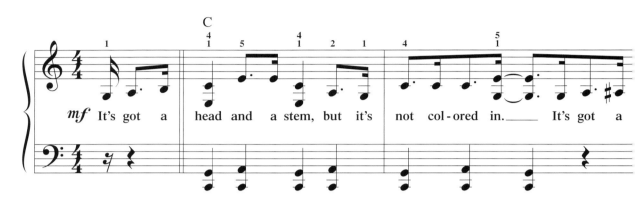

It's got a head and a stem, but it's not col-ored in.___ It's got a

head and a stem, but it's not col-ored in.___ It's got a head and a stem, but it's

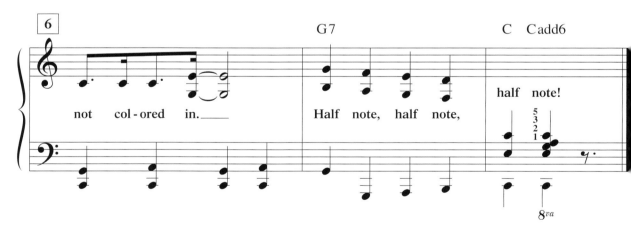

not col-ored in.___ Half note, half note, half note!

DUET APPENDIX

150

Musette in G

(Gavotte II from English Suite No. 3, BWV 808)

Student plays half and quarter note Gs HIGH on the keyboard along with the teacher duet.

Lesson Book p. 18:
The Half Note   Video 14

Johann Sebastian Bach

Andantino

I Like Duets!

Lesson Book p. 19:
The I Like Song   Video 15

Student plays The I Like Song on F-G-A high on the keyboard.

Mystery Position

Student plays The I Like Song on A-B-C high on the keyboard.

Spooky Position

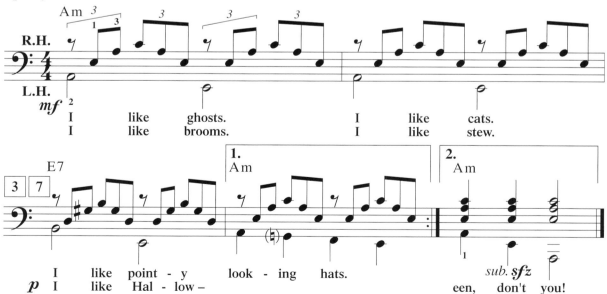

I like ghosts.   I like cats.
I like brooms.   I like stew.

I like point - y look - ing hats.
I like Hal - low –   een, don't you!

DUET APPENDIX

Student plays The I Like Song on G-A-B high on the keyboard.

Tooth Fairy Position

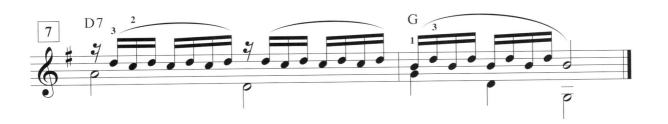

Let's All Tap It Forte

Lesson Book p. 20:
I Hear the Echo   Video 16

Student and teacher tap *forte* and *piano*. The student may also play dotted-half-note Gs HIGH on the piano with the teacher duet.

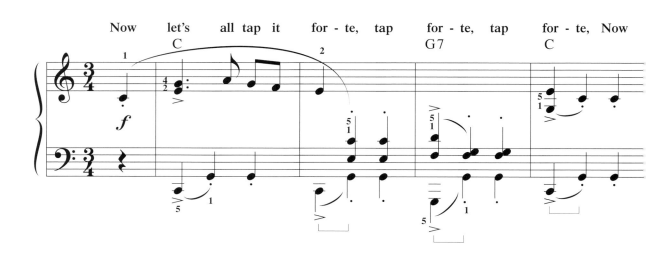

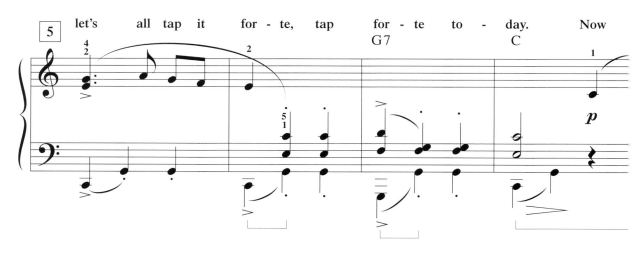

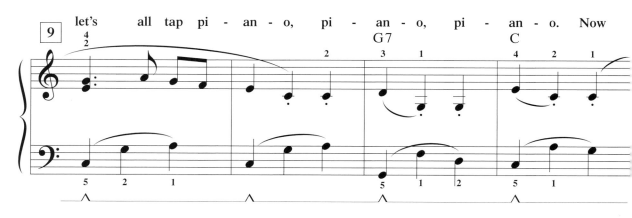

DUET APPENDIX

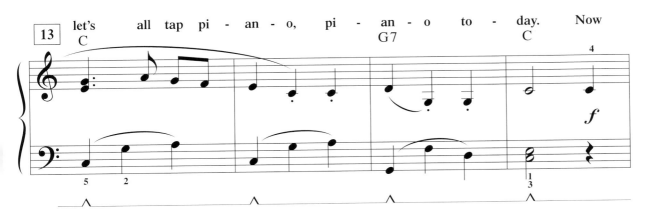

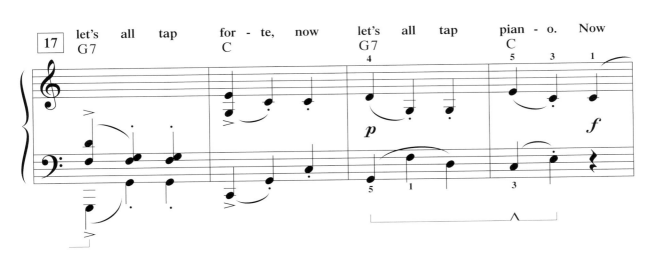

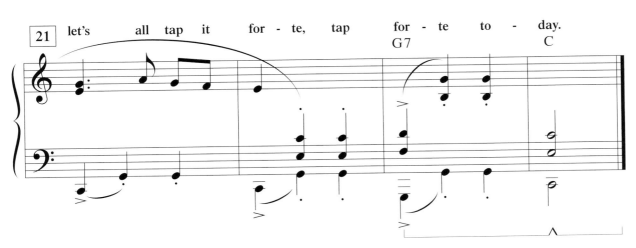

When the Saints March Forte In!

Lesson Book p. 20:
I Hear the Echo   Video 16

Teacher and student set a steady beat on Gs using braced finger 3s. Student continues as teacher plays at measure 3.

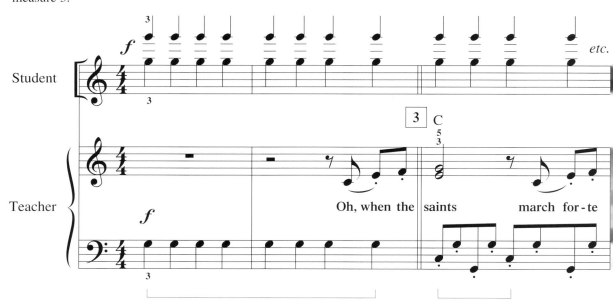

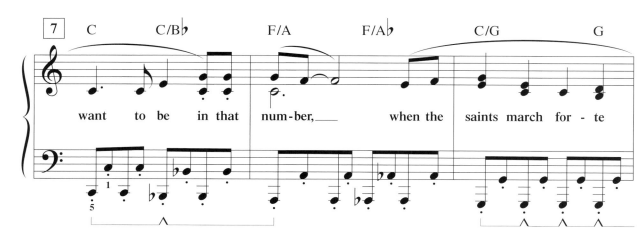

I Hear the Echo on the Moon

Lesson Book p. 20:
I Hear the Echo   Video 16

Student plays RH on the 3-black-keys, F#-G#-A# and LH on the 3-white keys, C-D-E.

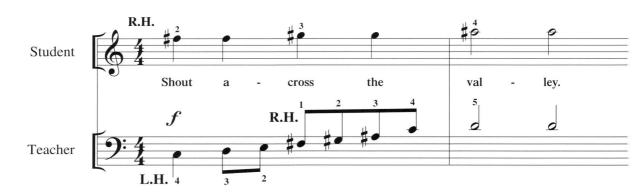

Student

Teacher

Shout   a - cross   the   val - ley.

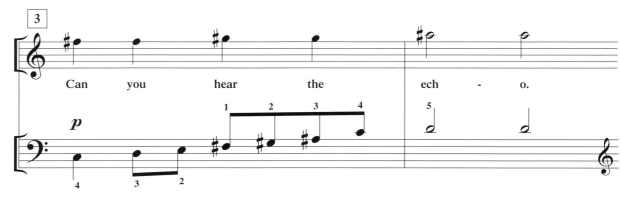

Can   you   hear   the   ech - o.

Play   the   mu - sic   loud - ly,

Can   you   hear   the   ech - o?

The Whole Note Song

Lesson Book p. 21:
The Whole Note   Video 17

Teacher and student sing. The student may also play whole notes on a HIGH G during the duet.
Have the student set a steady whole-note beat first, then begin the duet.

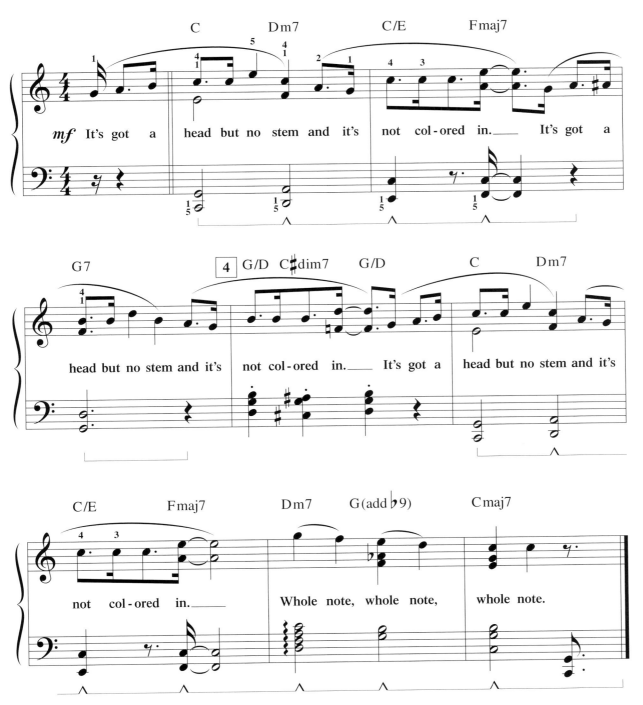

159

Old MacDonald Jams

Lesson Book pp. 22-23:
Old MacDonald   Video 18

Student plays Old MacDonald *high* on the keyboard.

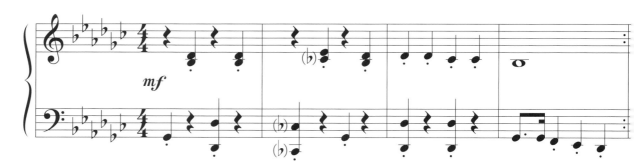

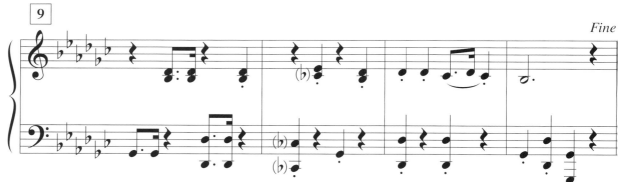

Teacher and student improvise "farm music" on the black keys.

D U E T   A P P E N D I X

"Back to the Farm"
D.C. al Fine

Jazzy Music Alphabet

Student plays rhythm by ear on A-B-C-D-E-F-G with teacher ostinato.

DUET APPENDIX

Jazzy Backward Rap!

Lesson Book p. 24:
The Music Alphabet   Video 19

Student plays rhythm by ear on G-F-E-D-C-B-A with teacher ostinato.

Balloons Floating Up

Lesson Book p. 25:
Balloons   Video 20

Student plays C-D-E up the keyboard.

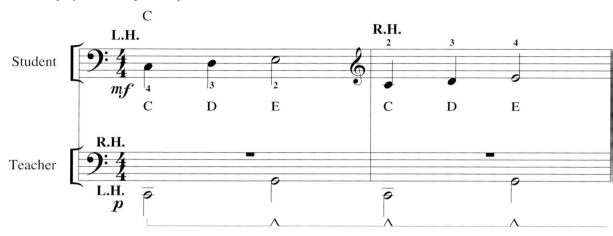

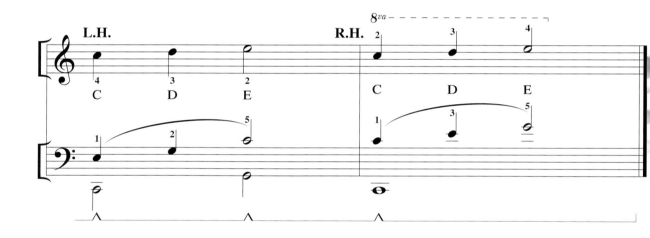

DUET APPENDIX

Balloons Floating Down

Lesson Book p. 25:
Balloons   Video 20

Student plays E-D-C down the keyboard.

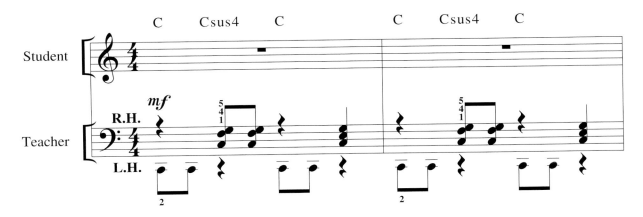

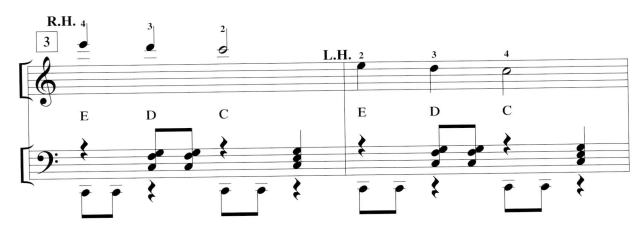

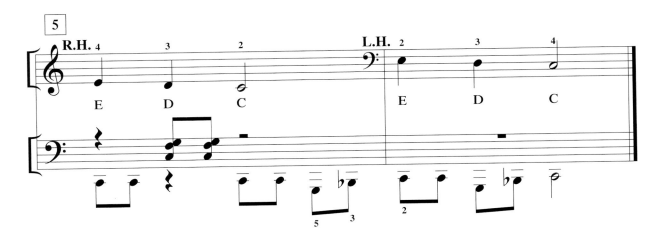

Merrily We Roll Along

Lesson Book p. 26:
Merrily We Roll Along   Video 21

8th-note accompaniment for Merrily We Roll Along. Student plays high on the keyboard.

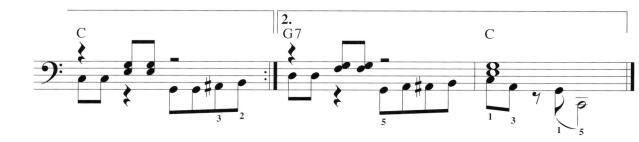

Triplet accompaniment for Merrily We Roll Along. Student plays high on the keyboard.

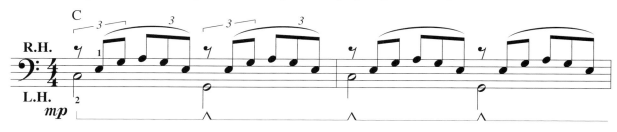

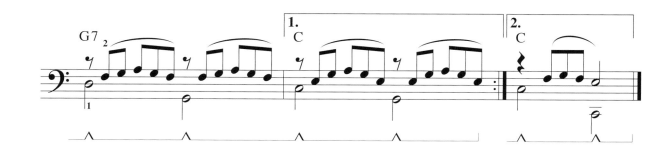

DUET APPENDIX

Scarily We Roll Along

Lesson Book p. 26:
Merrily We Roll Along   Video 21

Student plays Merrily We Roll Along on A-B-C. Student plays high on the keyboard.

C-D-E-F-G Rockin' March

Lesson Book p. 28:
C-D-E-F-G March   Video 23

Student plays in the middle of the keyboard.

C-D-E-F-G Outer Space March

Lesson Book p. 28:
C-D-E-F-G March   Video 23

Student plays in the middle of the keyboard.

BOTH HANDS 15ᵐᵃ throughout

DUET APPENDIX

The Half Note Dot Song

Lesson Book p. 32:
Hey, Mr. Half Note Dot!   Video 27

Chopsticks, Mr. Half Note Dot!

Lesson Book p. 32:
Hey, Mr. Half Note Dot!   Video 27

Student and teacher set a steady ♩. beat on Gs. Student continues as teacher plays at measure 5.

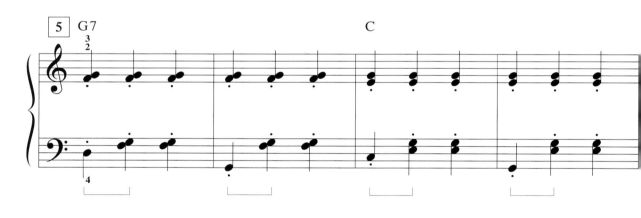

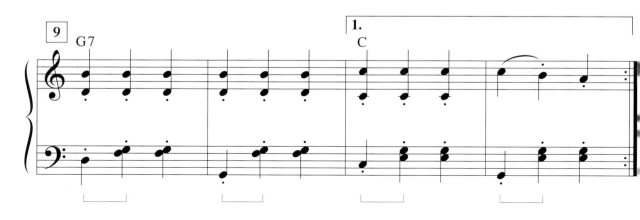

D U E T   A P P E N D I X

Line-Space Song

Lesson Book p. 34:
The Grand Staff   Video 29

Teacher sings or plays and sings as the student points to various lines.

D U E T   A P P E N D I X

She'll Be Comin' With Her Treble Clef

Lesson Book p. 35:
The Bass/Treble Clef   Video 30

Teacher sings or plays and sings as the student points to treble or bass clef.

Middle C Groove and Improv

Lesson Book p. 36:
Middle C March   Video 31

Student creates a new Middle C song choosing different fingers and rhythms.

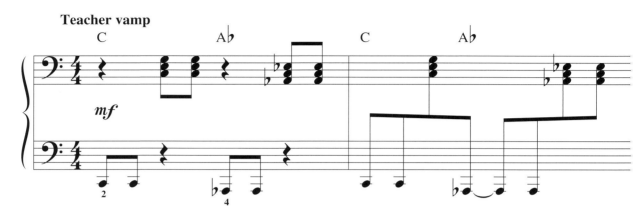

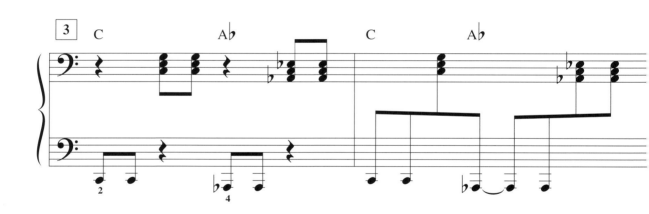

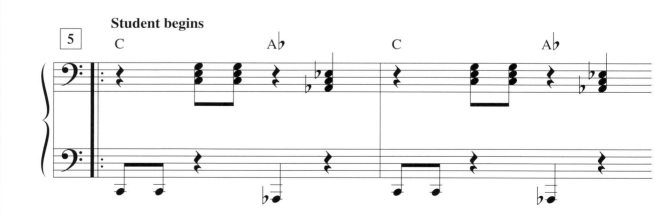

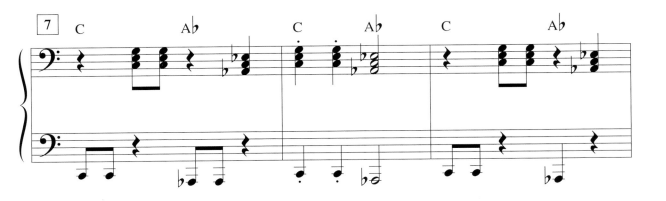

Repeat ad lib

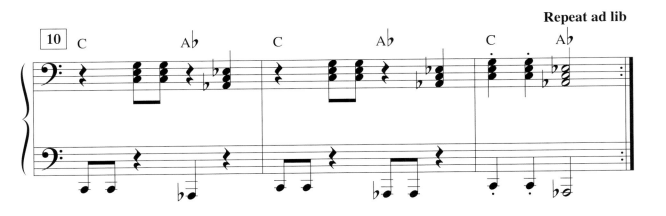

Ending

The Robin and the Traffic Jam

Lesson Book p. 38:
Driving in the G Clef   Video 33

There's a great big traffic jam. Horns are beeping. There are trucks, small cars, bikes that are ringing their bells. There's only one character that's getting through the traffic jam. Do you know who it is? It's a little robin hopping down the sidewalk!

Moderato

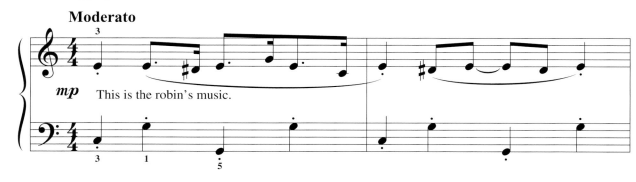

This is the robin's music.

All of a sudden, a big semi honks!

Can you make big, low semi sounds?

6 **Student and teacher freely improvise**
forte, **low semi truck sounds.**

Move it! Out of my way! etc.

But do you know what's happening to the little robin?

8

She's just hopping on down the road.

And then suddenly…

DUET APPENDIX

a car honks!   Can you come on around?

Student and teacher freely improvise
forte, **higher car honk sounds.**

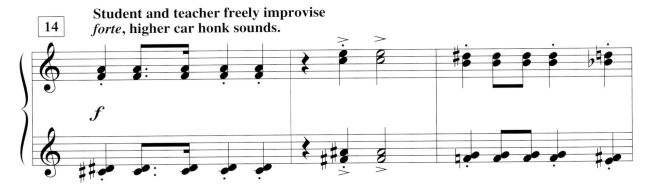

f

mp Who do you think this is?

And then a little bike bell rings.

23 Student and teacher freely improvise high, soft bike bell sounds.

p

8va

How about another semi sound?

27 Student creates *forte*, low semi truck sounds.

mp

ff And now everybody's honking!

**Student and teacher improvise
high bike bell sounds.**

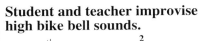

And the bike bell...

mp Who should get the last honk?

**Student chooses
last cluster to end.**

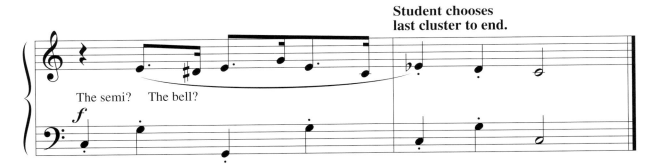

The semi?   The bell?

f

Dwarfs Dance to Student Ostinato

Lesson Book p. 42:
March on D-E-F   Video 37

Student and teacher set a steady beat on D-E-F. Student continues to play as the teacher starts improvising at measure 5 using the D Dorian mode (all white keys).

Teacher

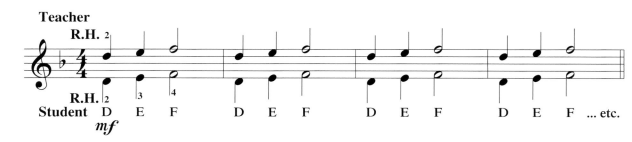

Sample Teacher Improv

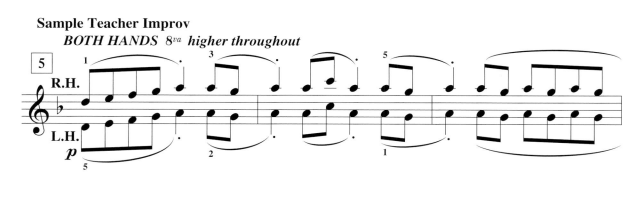

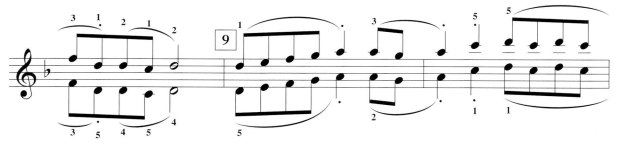

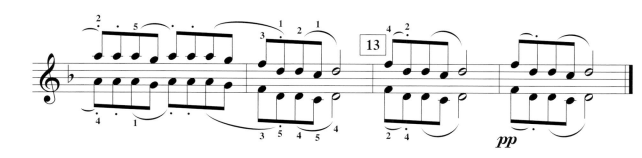

DUET APPENDIX

Student Improvises on D-E-F

Lesson Book p. 42:
March on D-E-F   Video 37

Student improvises using mostly D-E-F (with added C and G). Student continues to play as teacher starts improvising at measure 9.

Mister Bluebird and the Cat

Lesson Book p. 43:
Mister Bluebird   Video 38

Student plays Mister Bluebird (as written) along with the teacher, starting at measure 5.

Teacher Intro

p   The cat's waiting at the bottom of the tree. The bluebird's teasing the cat.

3

5   **Student begins**

DUET APPENDIX

Warm-up with C and B

Lesson Book p. 46:
Let's Play Ball!   Video 41

Student and teacher set a steady beat on C-B. Student continues while teacher plays duet.

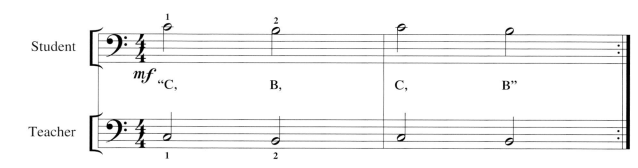

**Student repeats
using fingers 2-3.**

Alternate Duet for Let's Play Ball!

Lesson Book p. 46:
Let's Play Ball!   Video 41

Student plays Let's Play Ball! high on the keyboard.

Minuet in G Excerpt

(from the Anna Magdalena Bach Notebook)

Lesson Book p. 47:
Petite Minuet   Video 42

Teacher and student set a steady 𝅘𝅥𝅭 beat on Gs. Student continues as teacher plays at measure 5.

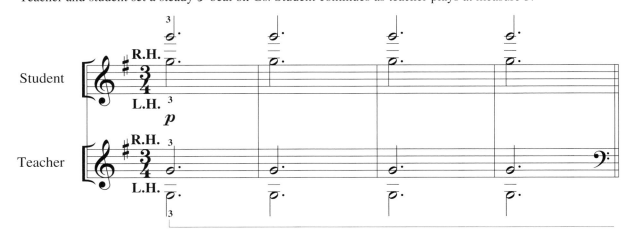

Student and teacher set the beat together for the next minuet.

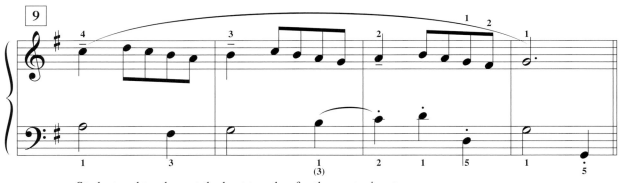

continue
without
pause

DUET APPENDIX

Minuet 2

Practice Routine for Rodeo

Lesson Book p. 48:
Rodeo
Video 43

Teacher and student repeat two-measure patterns as a practice technique.

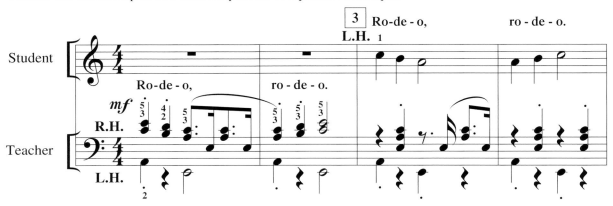

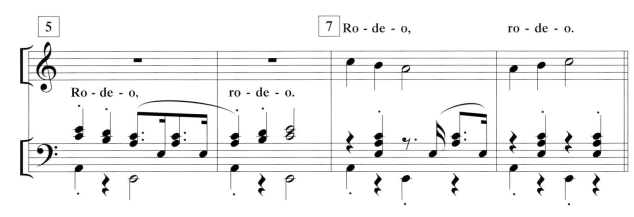

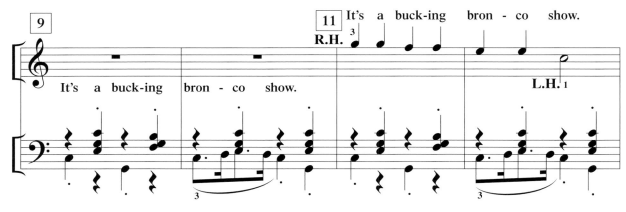

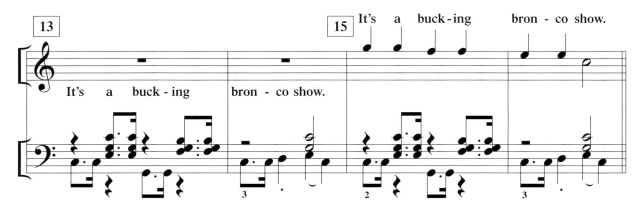

DUET APPENDIX

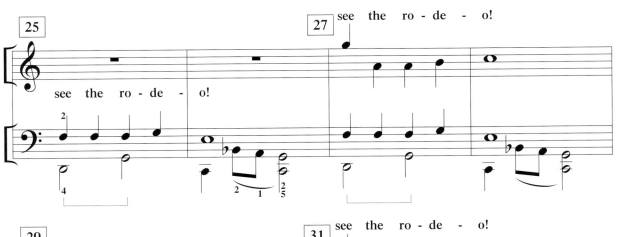

C-B-A Rodeo Ostinato

Lesson Book p. 48:
Rodeo   Video 43

Teacher and student set a steady beat on C-B-A. Student continues while teacher improvises in A minor.

Parade Medley

Lesson Book p. 50:
Come See the Parade! Video 45

Flag various pieces with sticky notes and create a medley using a simple segue. This example uses Mister Bluebird, Driving in the G Clef, and A Ten-Second Song. Student plays 1 octave higher.

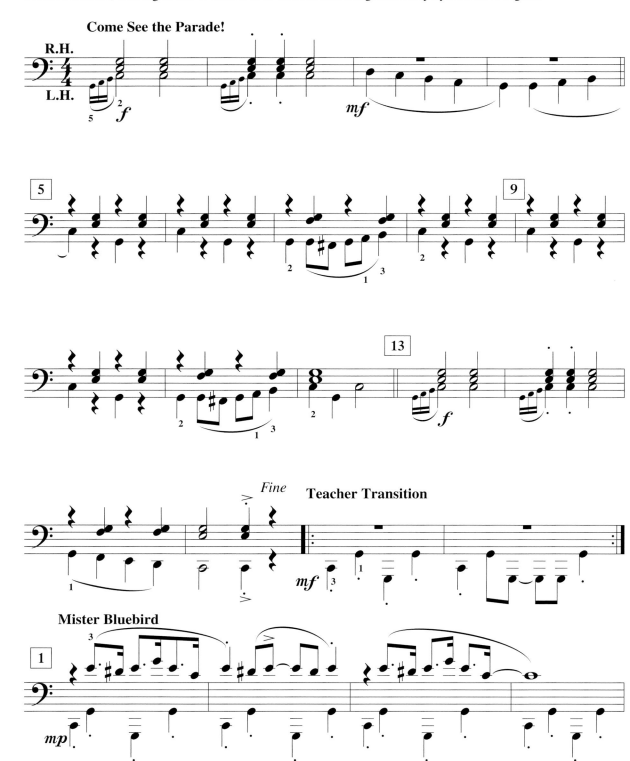

Teacher Transition

Driving in the G Clef

Teacher Transition

A Ten-Second Song

Transition to Come See the Parade!

D.C. al Fine

Hey, Hey, Pattern Up the White Keys

Lesson Book p. 52:
Hey, Hey, Look at Me!   Video 46

Student transposes Hey, Hey, Look at Me! pattern up the white keys.

Hey, Hey, Hear My Skips!

Lesson Book p. 52:
Hey, Hey, Look at Me!   Video 46

Student improvises using C-E-G skips with the right hand.

Yankee Doodle Goes to Town with Skips

Lesson Book p. 55:
Yankee Doodle   Video 49

Student plays Yankee Doodle, then improvises with G-B-D-F skips (LH 4-2, RH 2-4), then repeats the song.

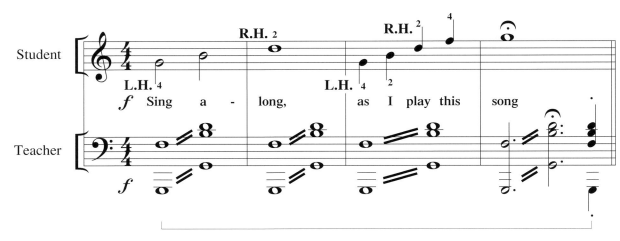

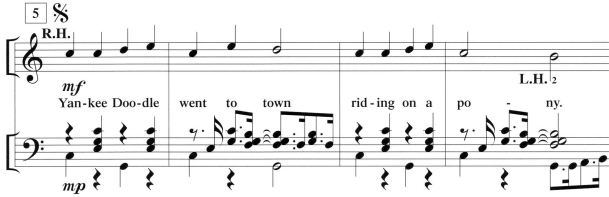

DUET APPENDIX

Raise Your Hand for a Rest

Lesson Book p. 68:
Come On, Tigers!   Video 59

Student closes eyes and raises his/her hand each time a rest is heard.

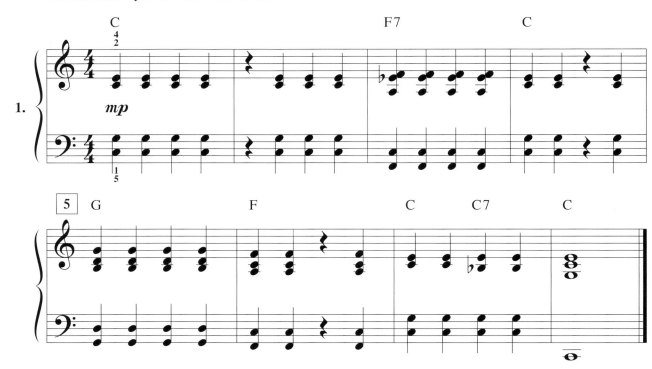

"Let's try an even trickier one!"

DUET APPENDIX

Cheer on C and G

Lesson Book p. 68:
Come On, Tigers!   Video 59

Student plays the cheer hands-together on C-G fifths.

Come On, Tigers! Duet

Lesson Book p. 68:
Come On, Tigers!   Video 59

Student plays using the LOWEST C five-finger scales.

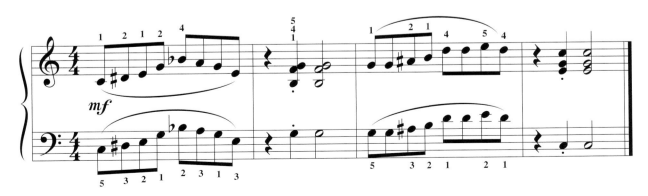

Once There Was a G Monster

Lesson Book p. 69:
Princess or Monster?   Video 60

Student plays the monster version in G.

Improvising with Skips

Lesson Book p. 69:
Princess or Monster?   Video 60

Student improvises with skips (1-3, 2-4, 3-5) in the C five-finger scale.

Super Duper Bugle Boy Duet

(based on The Entertainer)

Lesson Book p. 70:
The Bugle Boys   Video 61

Student plays The Bugle Boys as written while the teacher plays this duet.

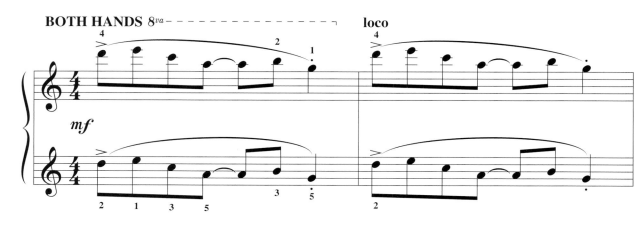

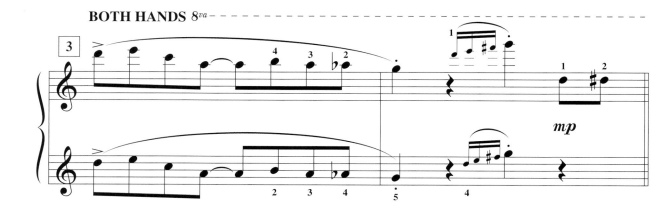

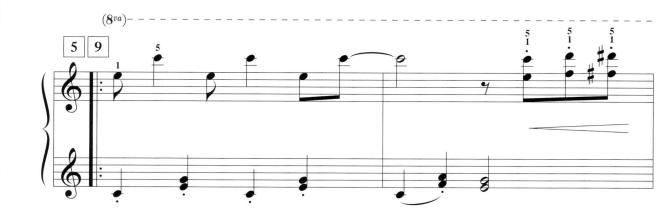

DUET APPENDIX

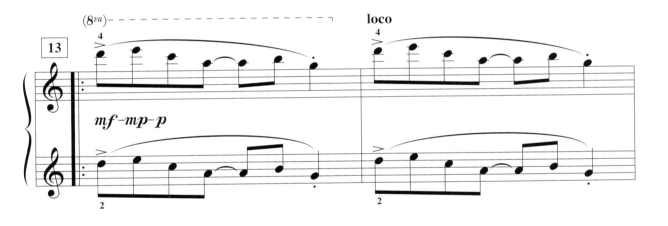

BOTH HANDS 8va

Play 3 times growing softer each time

last time rit.

Cross-Reference Chart

	Lesson	Theory	Technique	Performance	Sightreading
UNIT 1 Introduction to Playing					
Sitting at the Piano	4		3, 4		
Making a Round Hand Shape	5		3, 4		
Finger Numbers	6	2	3, 4		
Finger Flashcards	7				
The Pecking Rooster (for Left Hand)	8		5		
The Pecking Hen (for Right Hand)	9		5		
Two Black Ants	10		5		
Two Blackbirds	11	3	5		
Into the Cave	12	4-5	5	2	
Three Little Kittens	13	6-7	5		
UNIT 2 Basic Rhythms					
The Quarter Note	14	8			
The Old Clock	15				
The Walking Song	16				
Tightrope Walker	17	9			
The Half Note	18	10			
The I Like Song	19		6, 7	3	
I Hear the Echo	20	11		4	
The Whole Note	21				
Old MacDonald Had a Song	22	12-13	8-9	5	
UNIT 3 Key Names - ABCDEFG					
The Music Alphabet	24				
Learning C-D-E; Balloons	25				
About Steps; Merrily We Roll Along	26		10-11	6-7	
Learning F-G-A-B; The Escalator	27	14-15			
C 5-Finger Scale; C-D-E-F-G March	28	16			
Men from Mars	29	17	12, 13	8	
Ode to Joy	30		14	9	
Sea Story	31		15	10	
Dotted Half; Hey, Mr. Half Note Dot!	32	18			
Alouette	33	19	16	11	
UNIT 4 Orientation to the Staff					
The Staff and The Grand Staff	34	20			
Bass Clef and Treble Clef	35				
Learning Middle C; Middle C March	36				6-11
Learning Treble G; A Ten-Second Song	37	21			
Driving in the G Clef	38	22	17		12-15
Best Friends	39	23		12	
Learning Bass F; Gorilla in the Tree	40		17		16-21
My Invention	41	24-25		13	22-25

	Lesson	Theory	Technique	Performance	Sightreading	Gold Star*

UNIT 5 Middle C D E F G Notes

	Lesson	Theory	Technique	Performance	Sightreading	Gold Star*
Learning D-E-F; March on D-E-F	42	26			26-29	
Steps on the Staff; Mister Bluebird	43	27				
4/4 Time Signature; The Dance Band	44	28	18	14, 15	30-33	
Hopping Hand Position; Frogs on Logs	45	29	19	16	34-37	

UNIT 6 Middle C B A G F Notes

	Lesson	Theory	Technique	Performance	Sightreading	Gold Star*
Learning B; Let's Play Ball!	46	30		17	38-41	
3/4 Time Signature; Petite Minuet	47	31		18		
Learning A; Rodeo	48	32	20		42-45	8
Russian Folk Song	49	33		19		
Learning G; Come See the Parade!	50	34-35	21	20-21	46-49	

UNIT 7 Skips on the Staff

	Lesson	Theory	Technique	Performance	Sightreading	Gold Star*
About Skips; Hey, Hey, Look at Me!	52	36		22	50-53	4
Allegro	53	37		23		6
More About Skips; Elephant Ride	54	38	22, 23	24	54-57	16
Yankee Doodle	55	39	24-25	25	58-61	22-27

UNIT 8 Bass C D E F G Notes

	Lesson	Theory	Technique	Performance	Sightreading	Gold Star*
Learning Bass D; Magic Rhyme for Bass D	56					12
Learning Bass C; A Joke for You	57	40			62-65	
C Scale (Bass Clef); Football Game	58	41			66-69	18-19
The Octave; Octavius the Octopus	59					30
Copy Cat	60	42	26	26	70-73	14
Grandmother	62		27		74-77	
Musical Question and Answer	63	43		27		

UNIT 9 The Tie

	Lesson	Theory	Technique	Performance	Sightreading	Gold Star*
The Tie; Lemonade Stand	64	44			78-81	10, 20
All My Friends	66	45	28		82-85	36
Bells of Great Britain	67		29	28-29		28, 32

UNIT 10 The Quarter Rest

	Lesson	Theory	Technique	Performance	Sightreading	Gold Star*
Come On, Tigers!	68	46-47	30			
Princess or Monster?	69		31	30-31	86-89	
The Bugle Boys	70	48	32	32	90-95	34

*Correlations to the Gold Star
Performance Book are suggestions,
and the pieces may be assigned at
the teacher's discretion.

Music for Parties, R

tals and Special Projects

About the Authors of this Guide

Nancy and Randall Faber have combined their backgrounds as composer and performer to become leading supporters of the piano teacher and student. The husband and wife team has authored over 200 publications, including the bestselling *Piano Adventures®* method and the *PreTime®* to *BigTime® Piano Supplementary Library*.

Nancy Faber was named "Distinguished Composer of the Year" by the Music Teachers National Association for her award-winning composition *Tennessee Suite for Piano and String Quartet*. Her flute quartet, *Voices from Between Worlds,* was the winning composition for the National Flute Association's Professional Chamber Music Competition. Nancy's music has been heard on network television and on public radio. Teachers of composition include Joan Tower, William Albright, and British composer Nicholas Maw; piano studies were at the Eastman School and Michigan State University.

Randall Faber performs extensively as a classical pianist and lectures on musical artistry and talent development around the world. His performances have aired on television and public radio. He was a master teacher for the World Piano Pedagogy Conference, the Music Teachers National Association Conference, and the National Conference on Keyboard Pedagogy, and has presented as guest artist at universities throughout North America and Asia. Randall holds three degrees from the University of Michigan and a Ph.D. in education and human development from Vanderbilt University.

The Fabers advocate piano study not only for personal expression and performance success, but also as a vehicle for the student's creative, cognitive, and personal development. Their philosophy is reflected in their writing, their public appearances, and in their own teaching.

Marienne Uszler was editor of Piano & Keyboard magazine and is co-author of The Well-Tempered Keyboard Teacher (now in its second edition), Sound Choices: Guiding Your Child's Musical Experiences, and The Pedagogy Major in the College Curriculum: Undergraduate and Graduate Levels. Her chapter on keyboard music is included in the MENC Handbook of Research on Music Teaching and Learning.

For six years she was Editor for Articles and Reviews for American Music Teacher. Her articles, interviews, and critical reviews have appeared in The Piano Quarterly, American Music Teacher, Piano & Keyboard, and Arts Education Policy Review. She has given workshops and presentations throughout the United States, as well as in England, Canada, Australia, and Finland.

She is retired from the University of Southern California School of Music where she was Professor of Keyboard Studies and Director of Undergraduate Studies, and where she established the piano pedagogy program.